Kiel and Jutland

THE GERMAN BATTLE-CRUISER *DERFFLINGER*

Kiel and Jutland
The Famous Naval Battle of the
First World War from the German Perspective

Georg Von Hase

LEONAUR

Kiel and Jutland
The Famous Naval Battle of the
First World War from the German Perspective
by Georg Von Hase

First published under the title
Kiel and Jutland

Leonaur is an imprint of Oakpast Ltd

ISBN: 978-0-85706-593-3 (hardcover)
ISBN: 978-0-85706-594-0 (softcover)

http://www.leonaur.com

Publisher's Notes

Contents

Preface

We Germans are faced with a cruel fate. Our German youth will grow up in an enslaved Germany in which foreign Powers are compelling us to work for them. We shall see how the Anglo-Saxon will look scornfully down upon us. Even Frenchmen, Italians, and representatives of other races which are inferior to us intellectually, morally and physically, will pluck up courage to regard us Germans as brute barbarians, rightly punished for their crimes.

I am firmly convinced that our German youth will not allow all this to close its eyes to the truth. Brave Germans, old and young alike, must, and will, see to it that our nation does not lose its inherited characteristics in feeble, servile and un-German conceptions of life and the world. It is the duty of us elders to give young Germany the benefit of our advice and help in its approaching struggle. Part of that duty is to keep alive the memory of all that was done by the German people when it was proud and strong, and to recall the deeds and times in which it proved itself a true nation of heroes.

The twenty-two years during which I was permitted to serve the Fatherland as a naval officer gave me an insight into two phases of professional activity, that of the German officer and that of the sailor. Today, after the Revolution and our downfall have almost entirely put an end to those two sets of activities, I look back into the past with a feeling of gratitude to my profession in which I lived and worked all the time with men and boys who were German to the core and offered their lives and energies for Germany's greatness in peace as in war. I am particularly grateful to my profession for having brought me into contact with almost all the peoples of the earth under conditions which always left me proud that I was a German and a sailor.

In relating events from my old professional days my aim is to do something towards filling young Germany with the same pride in our

Fatherland which inspired us grown-ups before we had to draw our sword against a world of enemies. It was with that proud feeling that we were in no way inferior to any nation upon earth that we fought during four long years and stepped from victory to victory until we finally collapsed when men of our own race, essentially un-German, knocked our weapons out of our hands in the moment of betrayal.

In my little book I shall tell of two historic meetings between Germans and Englishmen.

The first was just before the outbreak of the war and was as characteristic as possible of the relations then existing between us Germans and our present mortal enemies, the English.

It was in June, 1914, that a great English squadron visited Kiel. I was appointed personal *aide-de-camp* to the English commander, Vice-Admiral Sir George Warrender, for the duration of the visit of this squadron. All that time, during which the Serajevo assassination occurred, I lived on board the flagship, *King George V.*, with the English Ambassador and other guests of the Admiral.

I wrote down my experiences and impressions of my stay on board the *King George V.* at the beginning of July, 1914, immediately after the English squadron left, using notes I had made in my diary every day.

The second historical encounter of which I shall speak is the Battle of the Skagerrak.[1] In the Battle of the Skagerrak, as the First Gunnery Officer of our largest, most powerful and swiftest ship, the battle-cruiser *Derfflinger,* I had the good fortune to be in the thickest of the fight, to take a personal part in every phase of the action, and thus play a decisive part in the destruction of the two English battle-cruisers, *Queen Mary* and *Invincible.* As at the moment there is no description of the battle in which one of the combatants gives an absolutely impartial and critical account, free from the shackles of the censorship, in recounting my experiences I have endeavoured to relate events solely from an historical and thoroughly unbiased point of view, and to describe the course of the action, as far as I was able to judge by my own observation, as it really developed.

But before I begin my story of these two historic encounters, I should like, here and now, to bring forward a classic example of something which shows that, in spite of all envy and rivalry, no true Englishman before the war ever thought of regarding a true German otherwise than as a representative of an equal and related race.

It was in June, 1913.

---

1. The Battle of Jutland. (Tr.)

Off the coast of Albania ships of almost all the nations were lying at anchor. The captain of the German cruiser *Breslau* had invited the admirals and captains of the other nations to dine with him. The English admiral sat next to the German captain, and around them sat Germans, English, Italians, French, Russians, Spaniards, Turks, Greeks and Albanians. A motley throng. There were toasts. The liveliest conversation on political events was carried on in every conceivable tongue. The English admiral and German captain caught each other silently examining the members of the "Round Table," and exchanged notes on the results of their observation of the various national types.

Suddenly the English admiral raised his glass, looked straight into the blue eyes of the German captain, and as the glasses clinked, whispered in his ear: "The two white nations!" With flashing eyes the two Teutons gazed at each other, the representatives of the two greatest seafaring Germanic peoples. They felt that they were of the same stock, originally members of one and the same noble race.

And before the war all true Germans and all true Englishmen felt exactly the same!

And now? The English people and their satellites now dare to call us "Huns!" The other of the "Two White Nations" gives our noble race, which has fought for right and freedom, hearth and home as none has ever fought before, the name of a Mongolian people of the lowest degree of culture!

German men! German youths! Do not let such foolish effrontery grieve you. Let us show our enemies in our daily actions that the culture of our nation is no lower than that of any other nation. Let us do all we can to teach the world the truth that we fought the war not less chivalrously than our opponents, and that it was their cruel measures only which compelled us to adopt stern reprisals.

VICE-ADMIRAL SIR GEORGE WARRENDER..

Kiel and Jutland

On May 22nd, 1914, *The Times* made the following announcement:

The Admiralty announce that four squadrons of battleships and cruisers are to cruise in the Baltic next month. All the principal ports are to be visited, including Kiel, Kronstadt, Copenhagen, Christiania and Stockholm. These visits are of a similar character to those which British squadrons have made recently to Austrian, Italian and French ports, which an Austrian squadron is now making to Malta, a Russian squadron made to Portland last summer, and a French squadron will make to that port next month.

They have been arranged between the respective Governments, and while they have no political or international significance, it is hoped that they may not be made occasions for anything beyond the customary exchange of hospitality which such visits must be expected to bring forth. These cruises will be most welcome to the officers and men, since they give relief from the routine of service in home waters and add to their knowledge of foreign ports. The last time a British naval force was in the Baltic was in the autumn of 1912, when the Second Cruiser Squadron visited Christiania, Copenhagen, Stockholm, Reval and Libau.

The following are the prospective movements of His Majesty's ships of the First Fleet, announced by the Secretary of the Admiralty:

The Vice-Admiral commanding 2nd Battle Squadron in the *King George V.*, with the *Ajax*, *Audacious* and *Centurion*, and the Commodore 1st Light Cruiser Squadron in the *Southampton*, with the *Birmingham* and *Nottingham*, will visit Kiel from June 23 to 30.

The news of the proposed visit of the English Fleet to Kiel caused the greatest excitement in Germany and all the world over. Some liked to regard it as an important step towards easing the political situation, while others saw in it nothing but a final bit of espionage before the inevitable conflict. The German Press soon became very busy with the approaching visit of the English Fleet, and the Navy made preparations for the reception of the ships at Kiel.

His Majesty the *Kaiser* commanded that two German officers should be assigned to the two English commanders as personal *aides-de-camp*. As early as May I heard that my name had been put forward for this duty to one of the English admirals, and at the beginning of June it was announced in Fleet Orders that I had been posted *as aide-de-camp* to Vice-Admiral Sir George Warrender and Lieutenant Kehrhahn as *aide-de-camp* to Commodore Goodenough, commanding the light cruisers.

During my service in foreign waters, particularly the Far East, as well as during a considerable period of residence in England, I had always had good relations with the English, especially with English naval officers of my own age. I had spent many a pleasant hour in conversation with Englishmen, and so it was a real pleasure, when I heard of my new appointment, to think of the social intercourse I anticipated with the English officers.

On Tuesday, June 23rd, early in the morning, the English Naval *Attaché* in Berlin, Captain Henderson, the navigating officer appointed to pilot the English flagship, and I embarked in a motor-boat, in which we went out to meet the English squadron at the Bulke light-ship, some ten sea miles out from Kiel. It was a rainy, thick day, and there was only a light breeze. At the Bulke lightship we met the six motor-launches of the navigating officers who were to bring in the other ships. Our little flotilla had just assembled when we observed two great columns of smoke away to the north. The English ships were approaching us in two columns. We soon recognized four battleships in line ahead in the left column, and three light cruisers in the right-hand column which was further astern. Seen from our low elevation the English battle-ships were an imposing sight. The dark-grey objects looked almost black against the smoke-grey background. On came the formidable giants, the greatest warships in the world. They were the celebrated Dreadnoughts, *King George V.*, *Ajax*, *Audacious* and *Centurion*, and with them were the light cruisers *Southampton*, *Birmingham* and *Nottingham*.

A signal was hoisted by the English flagship, which was flying the flag of the English Vice-Admiral, as soon as they noticed ours. The ships stopped, the engines were reversed, and when the mighty vessels had ceased to move our seven motor-launches went alongside the seven English ships practically simultaneously. We went along-side the *King George's* starboard accommodation-ladder and climbed on board. The ship's second in command, Commander Goldie, received us and conducted us to the Admiral, who was standing on the high Admiral's bridge with the officers of his staff. Captain Henderson introduced us to the Admiral. I welcomed him in the name of the Commander-in-Chief of the High Sea Fleet and the Officer Commanding the Baltic Station, and reported that I had been appointed his personal *aide-de-camp* for the duration of the visit of the English squadron to Kiel. The Admiral expressed his pleasure and thanked me very kindly. He at once introduced me to the officers of his staff, Captain Baird, Flag-Captain and Chief of Staff, the Honourable Arthur Stopford, Flag-Commander, and Lieutenant Buxton, the Flag-Lieutenant .

Vice-Admiral Sir George Warrender was a good-looking man. He was clean-shaven, and had an aristocratic face and fine blue eyes. He might have been about fifty, was just turning grey, but in his manner he had the elasticity of youth, and he was cheerful and kind. I had to draw up an official report immediately after the visit of the English Fleet, and in it I made the following observations on the personality of the Admiral and the officers of his staff:

Vice-Admiral Sir George Warrender, Bart.

Vice-Admiral Sir George Warrender, Bart., is a distinguished man of the world of the true English type. He is self-possessed and decided.

The officers of his staff and his ship have a high opinion of his qualities, and he is said to be very popular in his squadron, thanks to his personal character and his care for his men.

As we came into harbour, and subsequently, I was particularly struck with the way in which he—and, indeed, almost all the other English officers—settled all official questions. It was a matter of short orders and short replies, for which the English language is particularly suited. No superfluous words on duty. Thus, in spite of a general absence of military formalities in address, conversation and behaviour, the manner in which work was carried on seemed to me very sailor-like and professional. Warrender is hard of hearing, but the officers of his staff have had such good practice with him that he understands them even when they speak softly. He was in difficulties with the other officers and strangers, particularly when general conversation was at its height at table.

When I was with the Admiral alone, as when members of his staff were present, he made most minute inquiries about affairs in the German Navy, and was particularly anxious to learn about the conditions of life and service and the spirit of our officers and men. He also showed the liveliest interest in our wireless and petrol engines, particularly our submarine engines. It had become second nature with him and with his officers to compare their own navy with ours. Sir George Warrender frequently showed himself a superlative conversationalist. He knew some German, though he never spoke German in conversation. At his request I translated every day the German newspaper articles and letters which discussed the visit of his squadron.

Sir George Warrender is said to be a good tennis player and a splendid golfer.

He always spoke of His Majesty the *Kaiser* and His Royal Highness Prince Henry with the greatest respect. He was extremely pleased with the reception which His Majesty the *Kaiser* and His Royal Highness Prince Henry had given him and his wife. He always endeavoured to be exceedingly courteous to all German officers. To me personally Sir George Warrender always showed himself very kind and attentive. He frequently said how thankful he was that he and Commodore Goodenough had had German naval officers attached to them. As a matter of fact he used me exactly like a personal *aide-de-camp*.

Put shortly, my opinion of Sir George Warrender is as follows: He is a distinguished personality, who has his officers and men well in hand. He has a good head, is interested in and understands his profession, and his alertness is almost youthful.

FLAG-CAPTAIN BAIRD

He is Chief of Staff and Captain of the flag-ship in one. On his legs from morning to night, his principal function is to settle all questions relating to officers and men which concern the whole squadron (fetes, leave, sport, etc.). He looks somewhat worn out, but is a clever and energetic officer.

FLAG-COMMANDER THE HON. ARTHUR STOPFORD

He is the squadron gunnery officer. Has a clever head and a frank and honest nature, with special sympathy for German family life and customs.

Fleet-Paymaster Hewlett

Has a very confidential position. He comes before the Flag-Commander. His duties correspond entirely with those of our Squadron Secretary.

About nine o'clock in the morning of June 23rd we ran into Kiel Bay. It amused me to think that I, who had made this trip so often before, should now be making it on the Admiral's bridge of an English flagship. Off the entrance we ran into a heavy squall, but it cleared up as the storm passed over Labo and we saw the lovely harbour of Kiel lying in bright sunshine. A large number of yachts and naval launches circled round us, and the shore was black with curious folk, who had hurried up to witness the entry of the celebrated English Dreadnoughts. From Labo we were accompanied by the white motor launch of Prince Henry, who greeted us, with his ladies. The Admiral and Prince Henry welcomed each other with much waving of caps. In good order and showing splendid seamanship, all the ships made fast to their special buoys practically simultaneously.

Shortly afterwards we all assembled for breakfast with the Admiral. The Admiral had a very large dining-room occupying the whole width of the ship and panelled with mahogany. He had also a state cabin appointed very elegantly with light furniture. With all its cushions and its light carpet it looked just like a lady's drawing-room. These two rooms were for general use by the members of the Admiral's mess, though the latter usually spent their free time in their large cabins or the wardroom. For his personal use the Admiral had a large office, a capacious bedroom, bath and dressing rooms.

We made an excellent breakfast, and the Admiral discussed the arrangements for the day with me. Provision had been made for: 11 a.m. Exchange of visits on S.M.S. *Friedrich der Grosse*. Then report to Prince Henry. The Admiral asked me where I was to be found. I requested to be allowed to stay on the *King George V.*, which pleased him very much. He gave me temporary quarters in the state room intended for the Ambassador, and so my servant, Able Seaman Hanel, moved in with all my gear. It was a small, self-contained apartment, a cabin prettily appointed, bed, bath and dressing rooms. Unfortunately I did not enjoy it long, for the same evening the British Ambassador came on board, and I moved into a cabin on one of the lower decks, which was certainly roomy, but very uncomfortable and hot.

I lived and slept on board the *King George V.* all through the Kiel

15

week. As a result of my continuous contact with Admiral Warrender, and his officers and men, I had a chance of getting to know them well, and forming an opinion on their spirit.

In addition to the English Ambassador, the latter's son and a nephew of the Admiral, young Lord Erskine, were the Admiral's guests on board. At the time appointed we went in the Admiral's "barge," a very large and fine steam launch fitted up in mahogany, to the Fleet Flagship *Friedrich der Grosse*, where all the admirals and captains present in Kiel were assembled for the formal reception. Admiral von Ingenohl and Admiral Warrender presented their respective officers. The German officers adopted a cool and reserved attitude, and the English more or less did the same, so that, in spite of formal courtesies, the political tension could be observed.

In the subsequent festivities I failed to notice anything similar, especially in the intercourse of the junior officers, who were very soon good friends. At all the balls and dinners the young English officers could be seen getting on famously with the German officers and flirting zealously with the German ladies. A good many English officers were also invited out by our married naval officers, and so they enjoyed many an hour of German domestic hospitality. Many officers and men made use of the opportunity of free railway journeys which were offered them.

Every day hundreds of them went to Berlin and Hamburg, so that a large proportion of the officers and men were away from Kiel.

From the *Friedrich der Grosse* we went to the Royal Castle. We were received by Prince Henry, the princess, the young princes and the household. Their Royal Highnesses talked very intimately to the English officers. Both of them had a particular predilection for everything English before the war, and, indeed, among themselves hardly spoke anything but English. I had a long talk with the youthful Prince Siegismund and then with Princess Henry, who displayed a keen interest in what I was doing on the *King George V*. All the Englishmen were greatly charmed by the kindness and distinction of Prince Henry.

From the Royal Castle we went back to the *King George V.*, where meanwhile the two naval *attachés*, Commander Erich von Müller, who had come from London, and Captain Wilfrid Henderson, had arrived as guests for lunch. Commander von Müller drew me aside, and said: "Be on your guard against the English! England is ready to strike; war is imminent, and the object of the naval visit is only spying. They want to see exactly how prepared we are. Whatever you do, tell them nothing about our U-boats."

This information completely confirmed my own views, but I was none the less taken aback to hear the point put so baldly. I paid strict heed to his advice during the whole of the English visit.

The future was to justify Commander von Müller up to the hilt. He realized the approach of danger, even before the murder at Serajevo, so much better than his chief, Ambassador Prince Lichnowsky.

We had only been on board a few minutes when Prince Henry appeared to pay his return call, and he was soon followed by the commander-in-chief and the officer in command of the Base.

In the afternoon Flag-Lieutenant Buxton and I accompanied the Admiral on a round of visits. First we went to the Yacht Club, where Warrender had quite a touching reunion with his friend Rear-Admiral Sarnow, whom he had met in Eastern Asia long years before. For a whole hour we sat drinking champagne with the old gentlemen who could not do enough to revive the memories of bygone days they had spent together. Then we had tea with Admiral von Coerper, commanding the Baltic Naval Station, and afterwards went with him and Frau von Coerper to watch the tennis tournament for the Kaiser Prize on the square in front of the Marine Akademie.

When we went back on board we found that the English Ambassador, Sir Edward Goschen, had arrived and moved into the feudal stateroom, in which I had had to be content with an afternoon nap. During the next week I was to learn what a particularly kind and witty man he was.

He always treated us Germans with the greatest cordiality. He was descended from the Leipzig bookseller family, the Goschen, and was thus more German than English in origin.

After a short talk with the Ambassador we all shifted for dinner with Prince Henry. Full mess dress, *i.e.*, mess jacket with white waistcoat and gold braid on the trousers, was the prescribed rig. Just before eight we all went to the Royal Castle in the splendid "barge" in which we were to make many a trip in the next week. Dinner was a very jolly affair. We dined at eight small tables in the "White Room." In addition to the senior English officers, the admirals present in Kiel were invited with their wives, as well as a few members of the Holstein nobility. While the sumptuous banquet was in progress, a splendid orchestra played alternate English and German selections.

Soon after ten o'clock we again returned to the *King George V.* in the barge. With Stopford and Buxton I went into the wardroom, where I made the acquaintance of several officers of the ship. We spent a long and pleasant time together, drinking whisky and soda. The officers of the English ships almost always had two pretty large rooms for their common use—the officers' mess proper, which is used almost exclusively as a dining-room, and the ante-room, which is provided with club chairs and leather sofas, and in which the officers smoke, read and play cards. The furniture is the property of the officers. On the *King George V.* both rooms were furnished in particularly good taste.

The following programme had been arranged for June 24th: 10 a.m.—Visit to the Secretary of State of the Imperial Admiralty. 1.30 p.m.—Arrival of His Majesty in the royal yacht *Hohenzollern*. The English flag officers and captains report on board the *Hohenzollern* (immediately after she anchors). 7.30 p.m.—Dinner with the English Consul.

Lieutenant-Commander Kehrhahn, Buxton and I accompanied Admiral Warrender and Commodore Goodenough to the Secretary of State of the Imperial Admiralty, who had hoisted his flag on S.M.S. *Friedrich Karl*. Admiral von Tirpitz received us at the gangway and took us to his cabin. He there sat at a small table with the two English flag officers, while we juniors sat at another table with his *aides-de-camp*. English alone was spoken, as the Admiral spoke it very well. Warrender and Goodenough brought him kind messages from his many friends and acquaintances in the English Navy. Tirpitz then spoke of the development of the German fleet. Champagne was handed round. We remained about half an hour, and then returned to the *King George V.*, where the preparations for the reception of the *Hohenzollern* were at their height. During the whole stay at Kiel the men had no duties beyond keeping the ships clean. The result was that they all looked "tip-top." All the damage to the paintwork on the voyage over had been made good; the decks had been swabbed, and the space for the inspection of the crew had been marked off into equal distances with thin chalk lines.

At the appointed minute the *Hohenzollern* passed through Holtenau Locks. This trip marked the opening of the Kaiser Wilhelm Canal to public traffic. The work of widening it had been completed. Of course some dredging was still required before battleships could pass through, but this work was carried on at full pressure. On July 30th, 1914, the *Kaiserin* was the first dreadnought to pass through the canal. It was thus ready at the very moment the war began. The result was that when the fleet returned from Norwegian harbours at the end of July, Admiral von Ingenohl was able to distribute the battle fleet between its bases, Wilhelmshaven and Kiel. When the order came for the concentration of the fleet in the North Sea, the battleships from Kiel passed through the canal for the first time, though they had first to empty their bunkers. The fact that the war broke out practically the same day as that on which the canal was ready fulfilled a prophecy which I had made in the year 1911.

As I was firmly convinced that the mad competition in armaments of all the great nations would inevitably lead to a war some day, just as in the days gone by the creation of every fleet had led to its being used for war purposes, I prophesied to some merchants in Hamburg in 1911 that we should have war as soon as we had a high-sea fleet, consisting of two great dreadnought squadrons, with the necessary battle-cruisers, light cruisers and destroyers, in addition to a consid- erable number of U-boats, and immediately the coast defences we had planned, particularly Heligoland, had been completed. On August 1st, 1914, when the canal was ready, all these conditions precedent were fulfilled. The Dance I had prophesied could begin—and it be- gan! Subsequently one of the Hamburg merchants referred to the astounding accuracy of my prophecy. I must admit that at the time I had not thought that my conditions would be satisfied before the spring of 1915.

When the *Hohenzollern* passed through the Holtenau Lock, on June 24th, all the ships fired the Imperial salute. Several aeroplanes and a Zeppelin circled over the *Hohenzollern*. Unhappily one aeroplane crashed, and the officer, Lieutenant Schroeter, was killed.

The *Hohenzollern* passed us very swiftly. The *Kaiser* waved from the bridge of the *Hohenzollern* to where he saw Admiral Warrender stand- ing. The red-coated marines were drawn up on the quarter-deck of the English ships. The crews manned ship, and every ship gave three loud hurrahs, the men waving their caps at each hurrah. The bands of the Royal Marines struck up the salute. It was a magnificent sight, which I shall never forget.

The English officers were to be presented on the *Hohenzollern* im- mediately after she had been made fast. We therefore quickly shifted into full-dress uniform, and were quite ready to start when the Ad- miral reappeared on deck. The English captains had been told about the programme, but not one of them was in sight. We could see their gigs lying at the gangways, but not a boat moved. The Admiral was

GERMAN AND BRITISH FLEETS SALUTING THE KAISER AT KIEL ON JUNE 24, 1914

angry, and had the signal, "All captains to come on board the flagship," hoisted. There was quite a pause before the signal was understood by all the ships. Then, at last, all the gigs, pretty but slow boats, put off. It turned out subsequently that the captains thought they were not to come on board until a special signal was given. The Admiral was very much displeased, and I must admit that this want of initiative on the part of the captains was somewhat incomprehensible to me also. They had not used their fast picket-boats because there was a regulation that for official purposes the captain must only use his gig.

The Admiral's barge now quickly took us to the *Hohenzollern*, where there was already some excitement over the half-hour's delay. The *Kaiser* stood on the upper promenade deck to receive us. He was in high spirits and full of humour, as usual. Not one of the English officers failed to look anything but very pleased while the *Kaiser* was talking with him. As we were returning all the officers congratulated themselves on their good fortune.

After lunch, the Admiral, with Buxton and myself, went to the station to meet his wife. Lady Maud Warrender was a very tall and beautiful woman, of perhaps forty, the typical English society lady. I knew from the English papers that she was one of the leaders of London Society. She was known as a singer with a magnificently trained voice. She was staying on board the Hamburg-Amerika liner *Viktoria Luise*, which Ballin always sent to Kiel for the Kiel Week. This ship was the evening rendezvous of the social world at Kiel.

In the afternoon Princess Henry and her sons paid a visit to the *King George V*. Every spare moment I had was taken up withdrawing up the list of invitations to a great banquet on board the *King George V*. In this task I was helped by the Flag-Lieutenant of the High Sea Fleet and the *aide-de-camp* of the officer commanding the base. In addition I had to keep in constant touch with the English officers of the watch, the Admiral's secretary, the commander of the *King George V.*, and many others. I was frequently called to the telephone, which had been laid on the flagship, to give information to German officers and authorities. These were appallingly strenuous days for me, to the strain of which the excellent meals with the best of wine and much drinking of whisky and cocktails at all hours of the day and night contributed not a little.

In the evening of June 24th we assembled in the Hotel Seebadeanstalt, to which the English Consul Sartori and his wife had invited us. I had an opportunity of making the closer acquaintance of Commodore Goodenough and the captains. I was particularly impressed by Commodore Goodenough, the commander of the light cruiser squadron, who subsequently took an outstanding part in the war. After the Skagerrak Battle, in particular, Admiral Jellicoe emphasized his share in the action. As O.C. of the light scouting force he established contact with our main fleet, and is said to have kept Jellicoe always well informed of our movements.

This evening he showed himself a great wit in company. I also found out what a great conversationalist Captain Dampier, commanding the *Audacious*, was. *Inter alia* he taught me an amusing toast, which runs:

I drink to myself and another,
And may that one other be she (he),
Who drinks to herself (himself) and another,
And may that one other be me!

Most of the captains looked somewhat over-worked. One of the principal causes may be that the officers of the First Fleet live quite a different kind of life from that which we lead on board the ships of our High Sea Fleet. Service in the First Fleet usually lasts two years. During that period the ships are almost always either at sea or in different harbours. It is highly exceptional for the officers to have a chance of living ashore. Our ships, on the other hand, always return to their so-called "Main Base" after fleet exercises, and then we officers live ashore with our families, and during free times there are no officers on board except a senior officer and two juniors as officers of the watch. Thus we have plenty of opportunity of recuperating from the wearing life on board. The result of the unsettled life of the English naval officers (with whom, moreover, two or three years of foreign service are far more frequent than with us) is that most of the married ones cannot have a home of their own, but have to bring their families to the place where they and their ships are likely to remain for a considerable time. Their families then live in the boarding-houses, which are so common in England, or else they live somewhere inland, where their men folk can visit them from time to time.

In view of the fact that they spend so much time on board, the cabins of the officers are much larger and more habitable than ours. Most of them have a fireplace, as there is no steam heating on the English ships. The great leather club chair is a feature of every cabin. The mahogany furniture of the cabins is practically of the same style as that which was seen on board in Nelson's days. After two years on board the First Fleet the whole complement of the ship is paid off—a few particularly important individuals alone remain on board—and then the whole crew have six months ashore during which home leave is freely granted.

On June 25th the yacht regatta began. It had been preceded on the 23rd by the races of the men-of-war's boats. The bay was the scene of the usual sporting contest, the sight of which fills every seaman's heart with joy. Unfortunately the starting-point was too far from the *King George V.* for us to follow all the details of the start from on board. A very large number of yachts had been entered, particularly foreign boats. The *King George V.* was made fast to a buoy in the immediate vicinity of Bellevue Bridge. South of her lay the Fleet Flagship *Friedrich der Grosse* and the *Hohenzollern*, north of her the other English ships, and on the east the *Viktoria Luise* moored between two buoys. At 9 a.m. the 8m. and 5m. Class started, the 19m. and 12m. Class at 10 a.m., the 15m. Class at 11 a.m., and the Special Class at midday. Thus the bay was flecked with sails practically the whole day.

A comprehensive programme had been provided for the 25th:

Midday.—Lunch with the Commander-in-Chief of the Fleet.

Afternoon.—Three functions: Kiel Town sports, a *fête* on board the *Preussen*, flagship of the Second Squadron, and a garden-party at the house of the Mayor, Dr. Ahlmann.

Evening.—Invitation to the Kaiser's dinner on board the *Hohenzollern*.

Early in the morning came a note from Admiral Müller, Chief of the Cabinet, to say that the *Kaiser* would visit the *King George V.* at twelve o'clock.

At the appointed time the whole ship's complement was drawn up for inspection on the upper deck. The *Kaiser* came on board in the uniform of a British Admiral of the Fleet. He looked very happy and well and was apparently in the best of spirits. He was accompanied by Admiral von Müller and his *aide-de-camp*, Commander Baron von Paleske. All the English captains and the officers of the *King George V.* were present on the quarter-deck. Lieutenant Kehrhahn and I were on the left. The *Kaiser* asked Admiral Warrender to present all the officers to him.

When the Admiral was about to present us also the *Kaiser* said: "I know my officers," and gave us his hand with the words: "*Können*

Sie sich denn einigermassen mit den Leuten verständigen?"[2] The *Kaiser* did not inspect the ship's company, as is usual on such visits, but went immediately with Admiral Warrender to the Admiral's cabin, where he stayed talking with him more than half an hour. Before he left the *Kaiser* signed the Visitors' Book of the *King George V.*, which already bore the signatures of many famous people. He conversed for some time longer with young Lord Erskine, who had put on his Highland full-dress uniform in honour of the day, and then bade a very warm farewell to Admiral Warrender and the English captains.

Lunch with the commander-in-chief of the Fleet, Admiral von Ingenohl, passed off very smoothly. We lunched in the Admiral's cabin at small tables charmingly decorated with flowers. A special small orchestra played works exclusively by German composers. I sat with our first flag-lieutenant, and, of course, Stopford and Buxton. Ingenohl and Warrender both made very good speeches about the English and German fleets respectively. Indeed Warrender spoke twice and devoted the whole of his second speech to the spirit of good fellowship which had always existed between our navies. He referred to all the friends in the German navy whose acquaintance he had made in his professional career, and specially mentioned his friendship with Rear-Admiral Sarnow.

In the afternoon we had the difficult task of putting in an appearance at three simultaneous functions. With the help of fast cars and the good barge we easily solved this difficulty. First we went in several cars which I had had brought to Bellevue Bridge to the sports which the town of Kiel were holding in honour of the English crews on the town sports ground. The ladies watched the events from the stand while the Admiral went down with us among the competitors. Warrender had a wonderful way of talking to his men. He talked like a friend to the seamen about the contests and made them tell him what was happening. The events comprised a football match, a shooting competition, relay races, tug-of-war and so forth. It was extraordinary to see how our people won nearly all the events. We arrived just in time for the tug-of-war. Four times in succession the same process was repeated. With one irresistible swift pull our sailors drew the English crews over the line. The English could not claim a single victory in the tug-of-war. It was just the same with the other events. The football match alone was a draw.

I was not particularly surprised at the success of the German sail-

2. "Do you find you get on fairly well with these gentlemen?"

ors. Most of the English sailors were little fellows. Many of them were very young—the *King George V*. alone had 70 men under seventeen—while there was also an excessive proportion of old men. The tall Teutonic type was far rarer than among our men. Indeed, I observed that a large number looked strongly Jewish, a thing which astonished me, as I knew that the Jews had a fundamental aversion to seafaring.

From the sports ground we went in cars to Dr. Ahlmann's splendid place. Unfortunately it came on to rain, so that the party could not be held in the park in Düsternbrook Wood. We had to go into the fine rooms of the great house. There was tea-drinking, dancing and flirting. We did not stay long and then went by car and barge to the *Preussen*. The Base authorities had given me *carte blanche* as regards the use of cars, and that alone made it possible for the Admiral to meet all the demands upon his time.

Prince and Princess Henry were present on the *Preussen*, but otherwise it presented the usual picture of a fete on board. The decks were prettily decorated and we danced zealously. For the reception of the English guests the commander-in-chief of the Fleet had permanently assigned two Germans to each English ship, and the German ships were instructed to invite the English officers to lunches and functions on board. The result was that a large number of English officers were seen at the festivities on board during the Kiel Week. This was true of the *Preussen* also.

Introducing the Admiral to Kiel society kept me going the whole time. I knew so many people I introduced that he asked me in astonishment: "Do you know *everybody*?"

At eight o'clock in the evening we were commanded to dine on the *Hohenzollern*. It was the last banquet which was ever given on the splendid royal yacht. On this day the *Hohenzollern* showed herself in all her glory for the last time. We assembled on the promenade deck, where the *Kaiser* welcomed us. He was wearing—as we were guests—the simple mess uniform. The tables were set in the great saloon and decorated with superb orchids. Germans and Englishmen sat together in a gay throng. I give on the following page the order of the seats at this last great Imperial banquet on board the *Hohenzollern*. The letter B before the names indicates a British officer.

There were no speeches, but the conversation was lively. Indeed, the conversation on the Imperial yacht was always as unrestrained as possible. I had the pleasure of sitting next to Captain von Karpf , commanding the *Hohenzollern*, of whom the whole navy and particularly

Staff-Surgeon Dr. Wezel

Commander v. Müller

Capt. Begas

(B) Lieut. B. Buxton

Vice-Admiral Scheer

(B) Capt. A. Duff

Admiral von Ingenohl

(B) Capt. M. Culme-Seymour

Col.-General v. Plessen

(B) Vice-Admiral Sir George Warrender

H.M. the Kaiser and King

Ambassador Sir Edward Goschen

Admiral of the Fleet von Tirpitz

(B) Capt. William E. Goodenough

Admiral v. Pohl

(B) Capt. Wilfrid Henderson

Ambassador Count v. Wedel

(B)Commander the Hon. D. Stopford

Rear-Admiral Mauwe

Lieut.-Col. v. Estorff

Lieut. Kehrhahn

Lieut. v. Hase

Capt. v. Karpf

Rear - Admiral Hebbinghaus

Rear-Adml.Eckermann

Ambassador v. Eisendecker

(B) Comdr.E.A.Rushton

O.H.M. Baron v. Reischach

(B) Capt. Charles B. Miller

Admiral v. Müller

(B) Capt. Cecil F. Dampier

H.R.H. Prince Henry of Prussia

(B) Capt. Sir Arthur Henniker-Hughan

Admiral v. Coerper

(B) Capt. George H. Baird

Vice-Admiral Koch

(B) Fleet - Paymaster Graham Hewlett

Rear-Admiral Funke

Wirkl. Geh. Rat v. Valentini

Captain Hopmann

Commander Baron v. Paleske

Lieut. v. Tyszka

the royal family had the very highest opinion. He is well known for his splendid humour. We did full justice to the excellent food and the choicest of wines. Of one particular hock Captain von Karpf said that it was the best drop to be found in the *Kaiser's* cellars in Berlin. I noticed that the *Kaiser* did not get on very well with Admiral Warrender. Unfortunately Warrender also had the *Kaiser* on his practically deaf side, so that the latter talked almost all the time to the English ambassador. After dinner we had coffee and cigars on the promenade deck and conversation was merry and free. The *Kaiser* spoke to almost all his English guests. We noticed the way in which he devoted himself to showing himself to his guests as nothing but a kind host.

I had a very interesting conversation with the English captains Dampier and Sir Arthur Henniker-Hughan on the political situation and Germany's prospects in the world. Both insisted that England had no idea of isolating Germany from the world, but if war came it would be Germany that started it, not England.

It was pretty late when we returned to the *King George V.*, where we sat for some time longer in the ante-room of the officers' mess. It was on this occasion that I struck up a friendship with Commander Brownrigg, Gunnery Officer of the *King George V.* He told me many interesting points about guns, and in his cabin showed me shooting charts, the results of gunnery tests and gunnery prizes. We were at one in our mania for everything to do with naval gunnery. The English naval authorities knew how to make the career of the gunnery officer the most distinguished and coveted among naval officers. In the German navy the gun was a secondary, not the main weapon, and the torpedo arm had become the object of the ambition of every efficient officer.

This has always seemed to me regrettable, and I regarded it as a great mistake. The preference for the torpedo was justified when our navy was so weak that a battle for the mastery of the seas—which could only be waged with the guns of powerful ships—seemed to have no prospects from the start. Churchill said very aptly during the war, after the Battle of Skagerrak:

The first sea-power relies on the gun; the second is bound to place its hopes on the torpedo.

The fact that we put our hopes almost entirely on the torpedo in the war meant that to a certain extent we renounced the battle methods of a first-class naval power. It was only at the Battle of Skagerrak, almost two years after the outbreak of war, that Admiral Scheer, the Commander-in-Chief of the Fleet, ventured on an artillery action on the high seas, and that was after his predecessors, Admirals von Ingenohl and von Pohl, had failed to exploit any of the opportunities for a high seas action which had offered themselves so frequently.

Commander Brownrigg told me of gunnery exercises in which he had been successful at a range of 150 hm.[3] This seemed to me an enormous range. As a matter of fact, in the war itself, shooting was almost always at even greater ranges.

For Friday, June 26, Admiral Warrender had been invited by the *Kaiser* to sail on the *Meteor*. The large yachts started for their race at 10.15. As I was not accompanying him I was able to devote myself to the preparations for the great fete which was to be held on the *King George V.* in the afternoon. For the afternoon also, the Imperial Yacht Club had arranged a regatta for the ships' boats of the English squadron. In the evening we had been invited by the officers of the Baltic Station to a ball at the Marine Akademie.

Admiral Warrender did not get back until the afternoon. Meanwhile we had had a very pleasant lunch, at which Sir Edward Goschen presided and which was graced by the presence of several young ladies. The Admiral was delighted with the regatta, in which Rear-Admiral Begas had steered the *Meteor* to victory.

The "At Home" (on the King George F.), as the English call their ships' *fêtes*, was an affair of the first order. All Kiel was there and the invitations were issued through me. Of course some folk grumbled because they were not invited. Lady Warrender did the honours very skilfully and was supported by several German ladies, notably her friend, Frau von Meister, wife of the *Regierungspräsident* of Wiesbaden. The huge decks of the *King George V.* were unanimously approved by the German ladies owing to the large amount of dancing space they afforded. Borchert of Berlin had supplied the excellent refreshments, the splendours of which met with well-earned praise.

I made the acquaintance of old Lord Brassey, who was in Kiel with his yacht the *Sunbeam*, to which he invited me. He has written a famous book on his cruise round the world in this yacht. I was also introduced to his daughters, Lady Helen and Lady Mary. The yacht is rather old, but very large and comfortable. A few days later Lord Brassey had a remarkable experience. In one of the yacht's dinghies he went into the U-boat dock of the Imperial Yards, which was closed

---

3. 1 hectometre = 100 metres = 110 yards (approx.).

KING GEORGE V.,
FLAGSHIP OF THE ENGLISH 2ND BATTLE SQUADRON.

SOUTHAMPTON, COMMODORE GOODENOUGH'S FLAGSHIP.

to all civilians. There were several of our latest U-boats there. He was arrested by a dock-guard and spent several hours in the guard-room. It was only after he had been identified by a German officer he knew that he was released on the orders of the director of the dockyard. There was general indignation in Kiel at Lord Brassey's great want of tact, and even the *Kaiser* spoke rather sharply about it.

I realized the very day after the English ships arrived in Kiel that the English were extremely anxious to know all about the modern ships and craft of our fleet. Admiral Warrender sent me that day to our commander-in-chief, Admiral von Ingenohl, and I was commissioned to tell him that Admiral Warrender placed the English ships at the disposal of German naval officers who desired to see them. The Admiral particularly insisted that the German officers would be shown *everything* which they cared to see for professional purposes.

Admiral von Ingenohl was absolutely averse to this proposal and instructed me to present his compliments to Admiral Warrender and say that he regretted that he could make no use of this kind invitation, as he could not return the compliment, because, in accordance with regulations, we were not allowed to show many parts of our ships to anyone. I reported accordingly to Admiral Warrender, and the next day he sent me back to Admiral von Ingenohl with a commission to tell him that of course the English also had similar regulations, *e.g.*, the conning-tower, the torpedo-room and the wireless could not be shown. Everything else could be seen, and of course he did not expect that his officers should be shown anything contrary to orders.

It was not until June 26th that I received from Admiral von Ingenohl a reply by letter in which he said that I was to tell Admiral Warrender that "he thanked the Admiral for his willingness to show the German officers the English ships, and invited the English officers to visit the German ships."

Simultaneously Admiral von Ingenohl issued orders that the visits of English officers to the German ships were permitted, but that the regulations for the visits of strangers were to be observed. As these regulations absolutely forbade the visits of foreigners to our most modern ships—those of the Third Squadron, the latest destroyers and all submarines—the only vessels the English could see were the old battleships of the *Deutschland* Class. They certainly could not find out much about us from them.

The English themselves had prepared their ships—which were actually the very latest in the English navy for the visit of the German officers, by either removing or covering with wood all important apparatus, particularly all fire-control apparatus and the sights. Personally I was frequently shown most of the gear on the *King George V.*, although I did not ask to see it. Commander Brownrigg took me into the most remote corners of his turrets and magazines. It was only the famous Percy Scott "firing director" which all the officers shrouded in a veil of mystery. This was a device with the help of which it was possible to direct and fire all the guns from the conning-tower or foretop, a device which was the invention of the English Admiral Sir Percy Scott. Of course the English officers who showed me round generally asked me about our corresponding arrangements, but they did not get much out of me.

The ball which the officers of the Baltic Station gave to our English guests on June 26 in the splendid rooms of the Marine Akademie was a brilliant affair. For the flower-waltzes flowers were scattered in a riotous profusion such as I have seldom seen. It was a pure battle of flowers. We danced far into the morning hours.

For Sunday, June 28, we were invited to a luncheon given by the town of Kiel, and in the afternoon to a garden-party given by the officer commanding the Baltic Station. For the evening, Admiral and Lady Warrender had issued invitations to a dinner on board.

At 1 p.m. we found ourselves in the fine rooms of the new Town Hall of Kiel for the luncheon in honour of the English officers. Lord Mayor Lindemann made a speech on the English, and then Warrender followed with an excellent one on the town of Kiel, and everything else which had made an impression upon him. He described how the German officers had received the squadron in their motor launches and how they had come on board in the open sea. He even had a few grateful words for myself and all I had done. After Admiral of the Fleet von Köster, as a freeman of the city, had spoken about the English navy, Warrender made a second speech in brilliant form. Thanks to the many speeches and intervals in the meal, lunch lasted so long that we only just had time to get back, by car and barge, on board to change for the garden-party.

The historic garden-party of the officer commanding the Base, at which the Kaiser is always expected but to which he hardly ever goes, passed off very smoothly in brilliant sunshine. The only princes present were Prince Henry with his family, and Princess Marie von Holstein-Glücksburg. That year Prince Adalbert was absent for the Kiel Week for the first time. Moreover, the *Kaiserin*, the Crown Prince and the other Prussian Royalties had not come to Kiel this time as they usually did. I was assured from a well-informed quarter that the *Kaiserin* and the Princes had not turned up owing to the English visit. I considered this aloofness quite justified towards a nation whose Government had so frequently thwarted ours, for indeed the cool reserve of all Germans in high position had not failed to make an impression upon the English.

The garden-party was a particularly gay scene this year. We stood about, talked to everyone, and drank a cup of tea while the younger guests danced in the great hall of the house. Some ladies and gentlemen of Kiel society danced a *quadrille* (which they had practised beforehand) on the lawn. I took part in this. A large red carpet had been put down on the lawn behind the house, and here there were basket chairs for the most distinguished guests.

During the garden-party Admiral Warrender and his wife received an invitation to dine on board the *Hohenzollern*. The guests invited to the dinner-party on the *King George V.* were therefore released with the exception of a few of the younger ladies with whom we dined very pleasantly in the evening. Sir Edward Goschen again presided and got on very well with the German ladies, who supported him in his duties as host. After dinner we danced a little on the deck of the King George F., and then transferred to the Hamburg-Amerika liner *Viktoria Luise*, and danced there. The international character of the Kiel Week was even more obvious here than elsewhere. All languages could be heard. As there was very little room for dancing, owing to the crush, Stopford, Buxton and I collected a few nice people together, returned to the *King George V.* and continued dancing there. It was pretty late before the last guest left the ship. Thus the last day before the fateful day of Serajevo ended for us in the merriest association with our English guests.

Another very full programme had been arranged for Sunday, June 28. The Admiral and Lady Warrender were invited to lunch with Admiral von Tirpitz. In the afternoon there was to be a great reception in the Royal Castle, and in the evening we were to dine with the officer commanding the Base. Dinner was to be followed by a ball.

I was not invited to the lunch with Admiral von Tirpitz, so I lunched quietly at home. When I returned to the *King George V.* after lunch I was called to the telephone, and there received the order issued by the *Kaiser*. "Flags half-mast, ensigns half-mast, Austrian flag at main-mast, for murder of the Austrian heir." Admiral Warrender and

Sir Edward Goschen immediately came back from the *Hohenzollern*. Both looked very serious and the ambassador was in great agitation. I told them of the telephone message I had received. I stayed with them on deck for a time. Sir Edward Goschen had tears in his eyes, so that I asked him if he attached special importance to the assassination. He simply said that he had known the Austrian heir very intimately and loved him as a friend.

Goschen then suggested to Warrender that they should send a joint telegram to Sir Edward Grey. I therefore withdrew. When Warrender came on deck again he was even more serious. He told me frankly of the consequences the assassination might have. He bluntly expressed his fears—indeed his conviction—that this crime would mean war between Serbia and Austria, that Russia would then be drawn in, and thus Germany and France could not remain lookers-on. He said nothing about England, but before he had finished he said openly that this murder would certainly result in a general world war. I recorded this conversation in my official report, which I handed in on July 4, 1914. Even as we were talking together on deck Prince Henry came on board to bring us the news of the murder, and discuss it with Sir Edward Goschen and the Admiral. He was already in possession of some details of the murder.

The character of the Kiel Week was now revolutionized at a blow. The reception at the castle and the ball at the Base headquarters were cancelled. The *Viktoria Luise* received instructions from Hamburg to return there next day. The regattas were continued, but all dances stopped. We could begin to feel the thunder-laden atmosphere which filled the world until the outbreak of war. In the afternoon we learned that the Kaiser would leave next morning.

Very early in the morning of Monday, June 29, we left in the barge for the station, Warrender and Goodenough with their staffs, and Lieutenant Kehrhahn and I. The admirals and generals who had been summoned assembled on the quay side. Just before the *Kaiser* appeared Her Majesty the *Kaiserin* arrived. She had hastened from Grünholz by car, and was now to accompany the *Kaiser* to Vienna. She was all in black and looked as if she had been weeping. The *Kaiser's* launch came alongside and the *Kaiser* stepped out with his suite. He looked terribly serious. He received various reports and among them the notice of the departure of Warrender and Goodenough. He talked to both of them for several minutes. Then he had a long talk with Sir Edward Goschen, and spoke to the American, Mr. Armour, Prince Münster,

Admiral von Ingenohl and others. We all followed to the train to see them off. The departure was marked by a heavy silence, which was observed even by the numerous throng which had assembled notwithstanding the early hour.

In the morning the Admiral was present at the public funeral of Lieutenant Schroeter, who had crashed with his aeroplane. It was followed by an official luncheon on board the *King George V.* to which practically no one but the German admirals and their wives were invited. Owing to shortage of space only a limited number could be invited. Admirals von Tirpitz, von Ingenohl and von Coerper were among the guests. It was quite a simple meal, only distinguished from the ordinary daily lunch by a few good wines. After lunch Admiral Warrender offered to show the German admirals over the *King George V.* Curiously enough Admiral von Ingenohl accepted, while Admiral Tirpitz and the other admirals declined. Admiral Warrender took Admiral von Ingenohl and his officers (I myself joined the party) into a 34.5 cm.[4] turret and Commander Goldie operated all the machinery of the turret for our benefit.

In the afternoon I accompanied the Admiral alone by car to the dockyard convalescent home, where there was a sailors' function which was being given for our men by the English, as some return for the *fête* given in their honour. As Admiral Warrender entered the room he was received with thunderous stamping, a spontaneous act of homage which made a deep impression upon me. Warrender mounted a table as if he had been a boy, and made an enthusiastic speech about the friend-ship of the two nations.

It ended with three cheers for the German navy. Rear-Admiral Mauwe then mounted the table and replied. When he had concluded his speech and three cheers for the English navy had been given, Warrender gave him his hand, and thus the German and English sailors could see him hand in hand with the German Admiral in a somewhat theatrical pose. A terrific stamping, renewed time after time, was the answer.

At this time Warrender often spoke to me about the form which a naval war between England and Germany would take. I was particularly interested in his remark that it was owing to several articles by German naval officers that the attention of people in England had been drawn to the importance of Scapa Flow, and that preparations were being made to convert Scapa Flow into a base for the so-called

4. 13.5 in. (Tr.)

"long-range" blockade of the German Bight. His words were:

Scapa Flow is a German invention.

He and the officers of his staff often mocked at the well-known "submarine" letter of Admiral Sir Percy Scott in which the latter had said that the submarine meant the end of England's control of the seas. But even Admiral Warrender thought that submarines would effect a fundamental change in the strategic situation in the future, and that, owing to them, a distant blockade only, *i.e.*, in Norwegian waters, would be possible.

In the evening of June 29th the official dinner of the Imperial Yacht Club took place. Before it began there was the distribution of prizes, a duty which Prince Henry performed on behalf of the Kaiser. A large number of yacht owners and naval officers had assembled at the Yacht Club. I shall never forget how critically Warrender looked at every one of the young officers present, in order to gain some idea of his personality. He took quite a special interest in the officers of the submarine arm. He and his officers always tried to get to know as many of them as possible.

All kinds of interesting people were present at the club dinner, Field-Marshal Von der Goltz, Krupp von Bohlen und Halbach, the foreign naval *attachés*, and so forth. That night I slept for the last time on the *King George V* .

The departure of the English squadron had been fixed for June 30th. I was very sorry to see the end of a time which had been extremely interesting for me.

At their request I sent my photograph to Stopford and Buxton, who had always been most friendly to me. In return they sent me theirs. I also gave each of them some good hock. They replied by jointly presenting me with a very fine silver inkstand. They sent it from England on July 30th and it reached me at the end of August through the channel of the German Admiralty!

On saying goodbye, Admiral Warrender gave me a wonderful tie-pin, consisting of a large ruby set in brilliants. It was only in my possession a short time, as in August, 1914, I handed it over to the Red Cross. He also gave me his photograph.

I remained on board until the ship slipped her moorings. Then I left. Everyone was extremely kind, and I said farewell with feelings of gratitude. The fatherly, affectionate hospitality of the English Admiral I shall never forget, in spite of all the evil things which the English nation has done to our people since then, things which for the time being make it impossible for any self-respecting, honourable German to have friendly relations with an Englishman. The demand for the surrender of our *Kaiser* has produced an impassable gulf between us and the English.

I dropped into my launch and saw the ships leave the harbour at high speed. From the German ships the signal flew, "Pleasant Journey." As the ships stood out to sea, Warrender sent the farewell message of his squadron to the German fleet by wireless:

Friends in past and friends forever.

THE FORWARD GUNS OF THE *KING GEORGE V.*

THE QUARTER-DECK OF THE *DERFFLINGER.*

CHAPTER 1

My First Meeting with British Naval Forces

On December 15th, 1914, I witnessed for the first time a collision between German and English naval forces. On that day our battle-cruisers had been bombarding Scarborough, a fortified English port. I myself was on board a battleship, and had to be satisfied with seeing the *Hamburg* successfully beat off an English destroyer at daybreak. Just about the same time we had a meeting with our friends of Kiel Week which was extremely interesting, though for obvious reasons it has not been made public hitherto.

Our light cruisers had been attached to the battle-cruisers with the object of taking part in the bombardment. Unfortunately the seas were running so high off the English coast and the weather was so bad that it was impossible for the light cruisers to use their guns. Vice-Admiral Hipper, in command of the battle-cruisers, therefore decided to send the light cruisers back to the main fleet. The execution of this order was exposed to the great risk that the ships might meet a superior force on their way back. About halfway home our light cruisers came across a squadron of English light cruisers which were probably under the command of Commodore Goodenough. Owing to the thick weather the ships suddenly found themselves quite close to each other. The English flagship made an identity signal in Morse with her searchlight, and this signal consisted of two letters of the alphabet. This was read off by the German flagship, and replied to with certain letters also in Morse.

The English at length realised whom they were dealing with and opened fire, to which the German cruisers immediately replied. Thanks to the storm which was raging, however, hits were practically impossible on both sides. A thick squall came down in which the two sides lost sight of each other.

Almost immediately afterwards our six small cruisers ran into the eight Dreadnoughts of the English 2nd Battle Squadron, commanded by Vice-Admiral Sir George Warrender! With wonderful presence of mind, the commander of our light cruisers immediately made the English signal which he had previously noted. The English squadron was taken in and its officers thought they had their own light cruisers in front of them. That was the salvation of our ships, for a few salvoes from the 34.5 cm. (12 in.) guns of the *King George V.* would have been quite enough to send them all to the bottom. The two squadrons were only in sight of one another for a short time: then another heavy squall separated them and our light cruisers soon met our own battleships, in high spirits that they had successfully escaped so dire a peril. I think that both Admiral Warrender and his flag-lieutenant, Buxton, must have looked a bit foolish when they learned subsequently what kind of ships they had had in front of their guns.

Soon afterwards, Sir George Warrender gave up his command of the 2nd Battle Squadron, and was appointed to a shore command, undoubtedly because he had missed the one and only opportunity of successful action with which fate had ever presented him. In 1916 I read in a wireless message of the British Intelligence service that he had died while in command of a naval station.

The next bombardment of the English coast by German battle-cruisers took place on April 25th, 1916, and this time, as First Gunnery Officer of S.M.S. *Derfflinger*, the largest and most powerful of our battle-cruisers, it was my duty to direct the iron hail at the harbour establishments of Lowestoft and Great Yarmouth.

As soon as our bombardment of the harbour began two small English cruisers and about twenty destroyers ran out of Lowestoft, and after the bombardment was over a short running fight developed between us and these units. Unfortunately this action, in which we could easily have destroyed a large number of the enemy ships, was broken off after a few minutes, as the approach of a superior enemy force was reported by the light cruisers sent out to secure our flank in the south. Thus we did not get much satisfaction out of this action, though in the few minutes at our disposal we had set a small cruiser on fire and sunk one or two destroyers. The report of our light cruisers subsequently turned out to be false. Just as we were leaving the coast we were attacked by an English aeroplane which got so hearty a reception from our anti-aircraft guns that it left us, and, as I read later in an English paper, the officer was seriously wounded and only just succeeded in reaching safety on the coast.

In spite of our small military success against the English forces our raid against the English coast was none the less a very heartening experience. I shall never forget the moment when the high shores of England emerged from the grey mists of dawn and we could make out the details of Lowestoft and Great Yarmouth, and fire mighty salvoes from our great guns at the harbour works. In his book *Nordsee*, Gorch Fock has written about this voyage of April 24th and 25th to England in the "*Tag-und Nachtbuch, S.M.S. Wiesbaden.*" He was on board the *Wiesbaden*, the same ship on which he was killed in the Battle of Skagerrak. The splendid lines which follow will show what an immense impression this affair had made on the poet:

> About midday we make ready for sea, and all at once the whole ship knows that there is to be a raid against England, and that a great and solemn hour may once more have struck! A world power rushes out for its race with death, a mighty fleet. Here we are only beaters, and the giant grey torpedo-boats are only hounds for great hunters such as a *Lützow*, a *Seydlitz* or a *Derfflinger*! Beware, John Bull, beware! German wrath, the fierce, smiling anger of a Siegfried at Saxon perfidy, is about to break over you.
>
> ★★★★★
>
> How the ship trembles! As far as the eye can reach there are German ships of war, tearing, racing, wrathful hunters and hounds! Ever bluer is the sea, ever higher rise the mounting waves, ever whiter is the foam from our bows. How our wake flashes behind us!
>
> ★★★★★
>
> Rapidly darkness settles about us. Now we plunge forward into the night in grim earnest, raising great mountains of glistening spray. Pale stars gaze down upon us. The seas mount yet higher. Now and then a searchlight flashes forth. The destroyers can hardly be seen, but their white track of foam reveals their presence.
>
> The ship has become a mountain vomiting forth flames. All our neighbours are also volcanoes. An angry giant of superhuman powers has given vent to his rage. All the old gods have come

back to fight with us. Valhalla in the *Götterdämmerung*.
"Not a light to be seen on the seas! Almighty and primeval they menace us with the hammers of night!

★★★★★

A Zeppelin passes above our heads—a streak of shadow in the night clouds. There are stars. . . .

The rest of this diary went down with the poet in the *Wiesbaden*, in the Battle of the Skagerrak.

41

CHAPTER 2

The Principles of Gunnery in an Action on the High Seas

On the day of the attack on Lowestoft I learned a great deal which was useful to me, subsequently in the Battle of the Skagerrak. Several failures in the armament itself as well as mistakes of the guns' crews, revealed to me quite clearly once more that a perfect handling of the guns is possible only if all the gunnery mechanism functions faultlessly and the guns themselves are served without a hitch. It is only when the gunnery officer's instrument is working perfectly that he can obtain the maximum effect from his guns and their officers, gun-layers and crews can show that they know how to make a proper use of the complicated mechanical devices, mostly worked by hydraulic or electrical power, of their turrets, casemates and ammunition-chambers, as well as how to keep them in such perfect condition that however rapid the rate of fire their guns are always loaded and ready to fire the moment the fire-gong goes.

If this is to be possible a daily examination—which is in some respects a most laborious business—of all the electrical and mechanical devices is necessary and the artificers must at once put right any defects discovered. In this book I must give a special word of thanks to the tireless personnel of the *Derfflinger*. At the head of nine petty officers and more than twenty men of the gunnery mechanics branch we had our warrant officer Wlodarczek, who was known as the "goblin "all over the ship because he got things done even before they were thought of. He was my right-hand man and helped me most splendidly in achieving my aim. In the Skagerrak battle, there was scarcely a single failure in the mighty and complicated machine of the *Derfflinger's* armament which was due not to the effects of the enemy's fire, but to the incessant use of the gunnery mechanism which went on for hours on end. And what an enormous business the ship's armament meant with all its subsidiary paraphernalia. It had cost seven or eight million *marks* and improvements to the value of several hundred thousand *marks* more had been added during the war.

In the forward part of the ship, the forecastle, were two huge turrets, each with two 30.5 cm. (12 in.) guns. There were two similar turrets in the after part of the ship, over the quarter-deck. These four turrets with their eight 30.5 cm. guns formed the main armament of the ship. We called the turrets after the letters of the alphabet "Anna," "Bertha," "Caesar" and "Dora." "Anna" was the most forward of the turrets, "Dora" the furthest aft. Each turret had a turret officer who was either a lieutenant-commander or a lieutenant, but owing to the shortage of officers, turret "Dora" was in charge of a warrant officer. Our men had given turret "Bertha" a special name. It had been christened "the Schülzburg," after its turret officer, Kapitän-Leutnant Baron von Speth-Schülzburg, who was particularly popular with his men.

The secondary battery of the *Derfflinger* consisted of fourteen 15 cm. (6 in.) quick-firing guns, seven on each side of the ship and each of them in a splendidly armoured casemate. For other armament we had only four 8.8 cm. anti-aircraft guns (Flaks); the rest of them had been given up long before for our brave minesweepers and merchant ships in the Baltic.

The ammunition for these guns was kept in about fifty magazines which were protected against torpedoes by longitudinal bulkheads of strong nickel steel.

For all the guns I had under me three lieutenant-commanders, three lieutenants, four sub-lieutenants, four midshipmen, six warrant officers and about seven hundred and fifty petty officers and men. The whole ship's company of the *Derfflinger* comprised fourteen hundred men. As First Gunnery Officer I commanded all the guns, but in action I directed the main armament only. The secondary armament and the anti-aircraft guns were in charge of two of my officers, to whom I gave only general instructions for their tactical handling.

If the reader wishes to get an idea of the gigantic gunnery action which the Skagerrak battle mainly represented, he must be in a position to realize how it comes about that it is actually possible to shoot and score hits from a ship which is tearing along at top speed through high and stormy seas, a ship which pitches and rolls, changes its course, alters its speed, and is thus in motion in all directions. He must see how it is possible, at ranges of more than twenty kilo-metres, not merely to hit enemy ships now and then, but to destroy them in a moment! And he must remember that the enemy, too, is making the same crazy motions. He, too, is twisting and turning, pitching and rolling and making the same effort as ourselves to dodge the fatal shower of steel by repeated alterations of course.

At this point I must give a short description of what I consider necessary for a proper understanding of an action on the high seas if the reader is to get a true idea of the Skagerrak battle. In doing so I will start from the armament with which we of the *Derfflinger* fought in the Skagerrak battle. The armament to be found on all great modern battleships is very similar.

Our first object of interest will be the controls from which we officers directed the guns. The "fore control" was an armoured chamber which formed the rear portion of the conning tower, from which the captain, supported by the navigating officer and the signal officer, navigated the ship and conducted the action. During the action I was in this "fore control" with my three gunnery officers who fought the secondary battery, one sub-lieutenant, two men on the range-finder, three petty officers on the "director" (a secret gunnery apparatus of which I shall speak later), and five men for transmitting orders. Below us, but only separated from us by the iron grating on which we stood, were six other messengers and below these again in the so-called "pear" (the lower part of the conning tower was in fact pear-shaped) were one petty officer, two messengers and one gunnery artificer as a reserve.

There were thus not less than thirty-three men in my fore control alone! We were certainly pretty cramped, but quite satisfied with our station all the same. It was a splendid chamber, with armour protection of about 350 mm. of hard nickel steel which stood the test of battle magnificently. Even a direct hit from a 30.5 cm. gun at short range did not succeed in quite piercing the armour belt. The shock threw us all against each other and struck our shelter as if it intended to pitch the whole thing bodily over-board. However, we were all unharmed with the exception of a few slight wounds.

In action there were two other controls in addition to the fore control—the "after control," where the secondary gunnery officer, my reserve, had his post, and the "fore-top," usually called the "crow's nest." The "crow's nest" was in the foremast, about thirty-five metres above the water level. It consisted of a circular steel chamber in which the observer for the main armament, a lieutenant, and the spotting officer for the secondary armament, a warrant officer, had their posts, in addition to two messengers, and these observed the splashes round the enemy through splendid glasses and transmitted their position to us gunnery officers through their head telephones.

After the fore control, the most important part of the ship from the gunnery point of view was the transmitting-stations, two rooms down at the bottom of the ship. These transmitting-stations were under the armoured deck and therefore considerably below the water line; they were thus protected by the armour belt and the bunkers against hostile fire so far as it was humanly possible. All orders from the gunnery officers went to these rooms by telephone and speaking tube, and from there were transmitted by a very complicated apparatus to the individual guns.

It is necessary to determine the range very accurately before attempting to shoot at long ranges at sea. For this purpose we had seven huge range-finders which gave excellent results up to distances of 200 hm.[1] Our range-finding gear was all manufactured by Carl Zeiss at Jena, and was based on the stereoscopic principle. We had the so-called *Basis Gerät* (Bg.). Each range-finder had two "Bg." men. One of them took the range while the other read off the distance in hectometres and set the figures on a telegraphic indicator. The telegraph transmitted these figures to the so-called "Bg.-transmitter," an apparatus which automatically transmitted the figures given by all the range-finders. This "Bg.-transmitter" was quite near me in the fore control, and thus the average of the ranges given by all the instruments could be read off at any time. When the action began this range was given to all the guns by the gunnery officer.

As soon as the gunnery officer has made up his mind which enemy ship he intends to fire at he gets his periscope on to that ship. Periscope? some of my readers will ask in astonishment. It is the fact that the gunnery officers as well as the captain of the modern battleship no longer observe the enemy through a telescope or marine glasses, but use the same periscope as the sub-marine officer in his U-boat. At the lower end, *i.e.*, in the conning tower or fore control, is the eye-piece, while the lenses are above the roof. The great advantage of this is that during an action the small observation slits of the conning tower can be completely closed by armoured caps, so that we fight under a lowered visor, so to speak.

---

1. Hm. equals hectometre = 100 m. = 328 ft.

The 30.5-cm. Turrets "Caesar" and "Dora"

The 30.5-cm. Turrets "Anna" and "Bertha"

On the periscope of the gunnery officer there is the director, to which I have already referred, an extremely ingenious piece of mechanism which is of the highest importance in controlling the ship's fire. It has the following most astonishing effect. It enables all the guns of the ship which are connected with the director to follow every movement of the gunnery officer's periscope. Indeed, various devices on the periscopes enable us to train all the guns, some of which are as much as a hundred metres apart, on one and the same point, *i.e.,* in the direction fixed by the periscope, the distance of which has been established by calculation or registration. That is the point where the enemy is to be found! Thus where the director is at work all the guns are kept dead on the enemy without anyone working the guns needing to see the target at all!

The enemy may be near or far away. He may be right ahead or far astern. The ships may be travelling side by side or passing one another. As long as the periscope is on the target, and as long as the proper distance from the enemy has been established, every gun is aiming dead at that part of the hostile ship at which the periscope is pointing. Even when our own ship turns sharply the guns remain on the target so long as the periscope is kept on it. This is the duty of a special petty officer who keeps the periscope permanently on that point of the enemy which the gunnery officer orders. For obvious reasons I cannot say more about the construction of the director here. I can only say that the turrets themselves are not of course turned directly by the movements of the periscope. It merely operates an indicator in every turret which shows all the corrections for range and deflection. An indicator attached to the turret is kept permanently connected with the electric indicators when the turret moves; the turret officer follows the slightest movement extremely closely and it is thus possible to make the heavy turrets follow every movement of the periscope.

We now know how the guns are trained on the enemy. We know further how the first ranges are taken. The guns must now be raised or lowered according to the range, *i.e.,* the elevation must be adjusted according to the distance from the enemy. Owing to the perpetual variations of the range which changes several hundred metres every minute when the two opponents are approaching or going away from each other with the speed of an express train, it is not enough for the elevations to be given by the gunnery officer and then transmitted to the guns by word of mouth. The following ingenious piece of mechanism is required:

In the transmitting-station there is a so-called "elevation telegraph." When the elevation given is recorded on this telegraph an electrically controlled indicator on each gun moves to the figure indicated. There is another indicator on the sight of the gun. When the indicator on the sight moves in conformity with the electric elevation-indicator the proper elevation is transmitted to the gun. Once again the men serving the gun need not know how many hectometres the enemy is distant. The proper elevation is given when the two indicators record the same figure.

On the elevation telegraph there is another very important piece of mechanism, the so-called range clock. Let us suppose that the gunnery officer has established as the result of computations and calculations, which I will discuss later, that the distance between our ship and that of the enemy is diminishing at the rate of 750 metres per second. He merely gives the order "rate 750 minus." The man at the range clock now puts the indicator on a speed "minus 7.5." As the clock works the range given on the elevation telegraph gradually diminishes by 7.5 hectometres each minute. The indicator on each gun changes to conform with it 7.5 hm. every minute and yet there has been no necessity to give any orders.

Thus we have now a gun for which the desired elevation has been given and which is also trained accurately on the enemy. But owing to the heavy rolling of the ship it is pointing at the water one minute and up into the sky in the next. Yet it is obvious that the gun must be in the same position as if it were accurately emplaced on solid ground. As this is quite impossible on board, the skill of the gun-layer has to make up for it. In spite of the rapid motion of the ship the gun-layer must make it his business to see that the sight of the gun is *always* kept trained on the enemy.

Of course that means years of daily practice! And indeed it was astonishing what a high degree of skill our gun-layers had obtained. Shooting on a rolling ship was one of the most important features of our crews' training on the high seas. By the use of clever expedients it was even made possible for our gun-layers to practise shooting from a rolling ship though the ship was anchored in port. Small targets are moved about in front of the ships. Thus it is not the ship and her guns which move, but the target, which comes to much the same thing, as the targets move on curves which correspond to the rolling of a ship.

For a whole decade experiments had been made in our navy to replace the operations of the gun-layer by a cleverly constructed apparatus. Indeed we were actually successful! A complicated piece of mechanism like a top—an arrangement which certainly represents one of the triumphs of the human brain. It enables the loaded gun to fire automatically at the moment in which the telescopic sight is on the enemy. Further, this piece of mechanism allows for the amount of roll on the ship. It fires sooner when the ship is rolling fast than when she is rolling slowly. This is necessary because a fairly considerable time elapses between the moment of firing and that in which the shell leaves the muzzle. Anyone who knows how the rate of a ship's different movements varies will be able to realize with what a difficult problem our technical experts were faced in this matter.

But this is a digression, as I have been speaking of an apparatus which we did not have on board at the time of the Skagerrak battle. We did not get it until later. I wanted to mention it, however, because to a certain extent it represents the zenith of all gunnery developments for shooting at sea.

I must now refer briefly to the main armament of the *Derfflinger*. I said that the eight 30.5 cm. quick-firing guns were set in four turrets. Let us have a closer look at these turrets. The upper part revolved and consisted of the heavily armoured revolving turret and the revolving platform on which the two 30.5 cm. guns stood. The turret was turned by electricity. Close to the guns were the ammunition hoists, which also turned when the turret revolved. Behind the guns was a relay of ammunition, about six 30.5 cm. rounds for each gun.

We had two types of ammunition—armour-piercing shell and high-explosive. The armour-piercing shell was painted blue and yellow, made of the best nickel steel and had only a relatively small charge of high-explosive. The object of the armour-piercing shell was primarily to pierce the enemy's thick armour and then burst inside. Of course, in comparison with the enormous power of penetration, the explosive effect could only be small.

On the other hand, the high-explosive shell, which was yellow all over, had only a comparatively thin steel case which contained a large amount of high-explosive. This nature could not penetrate powerful armour, but had an enormous explosive effect on contact with unarmoured or only lightly armoured targets.

Our powder was contained in brass cases. Thus a 30.5 cm. cartridge looked exactly like a giant sporting cartridge except that the whole case was made of brass. Large cases such as these were very difficult to manufacture; they were also expensive and extremely heavy.

Notwithstanding these drawbacks we used these brass cases in the German navy even for the heaviest calibres, and in the war this practice preserved us, generally speaking, from such catastrophes as we saw in the Battle of the Skagerrak, with the sudden destruction of the *Indefatigable, Queen Mary, Invincible* and older armoured cruisers.

Of course we could not keep all the powder required for a shot from a large calibre in a brass case and so, in addition to the so-called main cartridge (in a brass case), we had a secondary cartridge the powder of which was contained in a doubled silk pouch only. These latter naturally caught fire much more easily than the others. But our enemy kept *all his* powder in silk pouches! Further, we kept all the cartridges which were not by the gun or on the ammunition hoists in tin canisters so that they could not easily catch fire, while the packing of the English ammunition must have been very defective. The immediate destruction of the whole ship as the result of a single explosion occurred only twice in the German navy—*Pommern* blew up on June 1st, 1916, on the morning after the Skagerrak battle, and *Prinz Adalbert* had previously blown up in the Baltic. Both disasters were the result of a torpedo hit.

The storage of powder, particularly cartridges, was of course a dangerous business for us too. With a view to avoiding catastrophes orders were therefore issued that only one secondary and one main cartridge were to be kept at a time on the platform by each gun, and the same rule applied to the lower tiers of the turret.

The revolving turret stood on the fixed gun turret which reached down through several decks and had the armoured deck as its base. The interior was divided into several tiers—the transfer room, the switch room, the magazine and the cartridge magazine, *i.e.*, including the gun platform, five stories, in which the turret complement of 70 or 80 men were distributed. In the magazine and cartridge magazine the lower ammunition hoists—which ran up to the transfer room— were loaded.

The function of the transfer room was to send up the ammunition to the guns. We had no hoists running right through; they connected in the transfer room. The business of transfer delayed the process (in itself) of sending the shell or cartridge from the magazine to the gun. But on the other hand two rounds of cartridges for each gun were simultaneously on their way.

The fact that a small stock of ammunition and cartridges was kept in the transfer room meant that the latter, and not the magazine and cartridge magazine, became the reservoir from which the gun was supplied. The vital factor for the supply of ammunition to the gun was thus the time taken by the upper hoists in sending up ammunition from the transfer room to the gun, a time only half of the whole period required for the passage from the magazine to the gun. We could fire comfortably with each gun every thirty seconds. Thus each turret, even if only one of the two guns were used, could fire a round every fifteen seconds. In the Battle of the Skagerrak I fired a salvo of four rounds—one from each turret—every twenty seconds for a considerable time, a thing which would have been impossible with the continuous ammunition hoists such as the older ships possessed.

The transfer room contained in addition to the apparatus for the ammunition supply the hydraulic pumps for the elevating gear and much other machinery. In the switch room were the switch-boards for all the electrical machinery in the turret. In the magazine was all the machinery for sending up the ammunition, most of it being electrically driven. A 30.5 shell weighed about 400 kg.[2] and a cartridge about 150 kg.[2]

The complement of a turret comprised 1 lieutenant-commander or lieutenant as turret officer, 1 *Stückmeister*[3] to work the turret and 75 petty officers and men. These were distributed as follows: On the gun platform there were 4 petty officers and 20 men to serve the gun, as well as a few messengers and range-takers. In the transfer room there were 1 petty officer and 12 men, in the switch room 1 warrant officer and 3 men of the gunnery mechanics branch; in the magazines 1 petty officer and about 18 men, and in the cartridge magazines 1 petty officer and about 14 men. This turret complement was swelled in action by about 12 men as a reserve: they usually took the places of men on leave or on the sick list. Thus the main armament had a total complement of about 350, not reckoning 25 messengers.

The serving of the 15 cm. guns was a more simple matter. Each gun, which was laid by hand, was served by 10 men in the casemate, while there were 4 or 5 men in each 15 cm. magazine. That meant 15 men for each gun and therefore a complement of 210 for the secondary armament, not counting 20 messengers.

I am afraid I have already tormented the reader too long with the detailed description of gunnery apparatus, so I will stop for the

---

2. About 8 cwt. and 3 cwt. respectively.
3. No English equivalent.

time being. When I come to deal with the gun duel in the Skager-rak battle I shall have to refer to a few ingenious instruments which were invented to facilitate fire control and, above all, relieve the officer responsible of some of the business of calculation which fire control requires (continually) in shooting at high speed and where both one's own ships and those of the enemy are continually changing course.

As I have said before, Lowestoft and Great Yarmouth left us with a feeling of great dissatisfaction. After Lowestoft I was possessed by a burning desire to engage our proud *Derfflinger* in action with an English battle-cruiser worthy of her. Day and night this thought never left me. I pictured to myself how, on outpost duty or one of our recon-naissances, we came across an English battle-cruiser, how the Derf-flinger joined action and thus a gigantic gun duel developed while we both tore along at a delirious speed. I could see how every salvo from the enemy was replied to by one from us, how the fight became ever faster and more furious, and how we struggled together like two mighty warriors who both know well enough that "only one of us will survive."

In my dreams I saw the English gunnery officer get his periscope on to my ship: I heard his English orders and my own. This thought of such a contest between giant ships intoxicated me, and my im-agination painted pictures of monstrous happenings. Previously I had regarded our target practice as a kind of sport and done my best to get hold of my officers and men through their sporting ambitions. In peace we had seen many a strenuous competition between the ships of a single squadron in trying to secure the largest possible number of hits on one of the old, obsolete battleships which lay anchored as a so-called target in some shallow place off Kiel Bay: or when our exercise was night-firing at destroyers which were represented by low targets which were painted black and towed. Many a time whole squadrons had fired at a squadron of targets, each ship having her own target. There had been the fiercest rivalry between the gunnery officers to score the most hits. This sporting spirit was less conspicuous in war and I missed it sorely.

And now I dreamed of a sporting contest more gigantic than I could ever have imagined. We should face our opponent with the same weapons and the duel would decide which of us knew his business best and which of us possessed the better weapons and the stronger nerves. My longing for such a duel was such that the idea of the danger to life it involved seemed to me something wholly secondary. Such a battle would at the same time mean an awakening from the lethargy in which we sailors threatened to sink as the result of the inaction of our fleet in comparison with the glorious feats of our army.

CHAPTER 3

The Tactical Principles of a Naval Action on the High Seas

A few days ago a regular captain in the army asked me: "Do fleets really lie at anchor in a naval battle, or do they steam all the time?" Again, other men particularly well informed on military affairs have often assured me that they had not the slightest notion of naval tactics.

As I have not written this book for my old comrades alone, but primarily for the largest possible number of German boys (who are likely, alas, to grow up with piteously little notion of sailoring, particularly such knowledge as can only be gained on the high seas), may I be allowed to say something about the way in which ships are brought into contact with the enemy?

Of course, there is no such thing as anchoring the fleets a certain distance apart and then beginning a gun duel. Quite the reverse. It may be assumed that during a naval action every ship is always steaming at the highest speed she can, by hook or crook, develop. It is scarcely possible to compare a naval battle with any form of operation on land. An aerial battle between squadrons of aeroplanes is the nearest approach. Perhaps the war of the future will unfold battle pictures which will not be altogether unlike a naval action—masses of giant, heavily-armoured tanks rushing to meet each other, with the speed of racing cars, trying to get round each other, to secure the better tactical position by manoeuvring and finally to force a decision by a fierce artillery and aerial-torpedo action at long and close ranges.

With a ship, "action speed" is the same thing as "maximum speed." This is simply due to the fact that on a great waste of waters such as the high seas there are certain tactically favourable positions which both the two adversaries would like to have secured when real contact is established and the gun duel begins, positions which both of them desire to reach or maintain during the action. The determining elements for the value of a position are the direction of the wind, sun, the amount of sea and visibility.

It is unfavourable if the smoke from one's own guns hangs in front of them, i.e., "clings" to the ship, or drifts towards the enemy's line. It is bad if the enemy has the sun behind him, because in that case our gun-layers will be dazzled and the silhouettes of the hostile ships will be far less sharp. It is also unfavourable if we have to shoot right towards a high rolling sea, which means that the spray often comes over the guns and makes things difficult for the gun-layer at the telescopic sight, as well as for the gun's crew. Lastly, visibility and light may be of paramount importance, as these may vary so greatly in different quarters that it may happen that we can easily see the enemy ship, ourselves being concealed as completely from the enemy as if we were shrouded in the hood of invisibility.

Apart from these tactical advantages, which are to a certain extent local, there are tactical points which have advantages purely as such, and arise out of the position of the ships. For example, if a ship has the enemy ship at right-angles to her bows, the latter can use all the guns of her broadside, and in a modern ship that means all the main armament and half the secondary armament. The former, on the other hand, which has her opponent across her bows, can only use one or two turrets against the enemy. Both broad-sides of the secondary armament and half the main armament can play no part. Every ship will thus always move heaven and earth to avoid this so-called "T position," in which the ship steaming along the horizontal limb of the T enjoys a great advantage. The English call it "Crossing the T."

Even whole squadrons and fleets may find themselves in this T position. It has always been the aim of the faster ships to get *across* the head of the enemy column in order to "enfilade" it, i.e., get it under fire from ahead, or, at any rate, force it back. If the leading ships of a fleet are well headed off, the line of this whole fleet will gradually become circular, the circle will get smaller and smaller and at last the fleet finds itself in the so-called "caldron."

Of course this can only happen to a fleet which is very materially inferior in speed or is surprised by the sudden appearance of new hostile units on its own course. Exactly what happened to us at the Battle of Skagerrak! Our fleet ended up by butting into the very

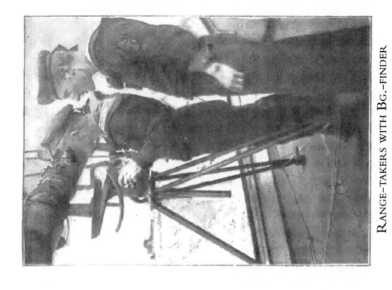

RANGE-TAKERS WITH Bg.-FINDER

THE FORE-TOP OR CROW'S NEST

centre of the enemy's fleet, which was forming a semicircle around us; it would thus have been exposed to the murderous fire of the whole hostile fleet, and soon lost all power to manoeuvre if—but I will not anticipate. We must not go through all that until we get to the turmoil of the action itself.

At the moment I shall only ask to be permitted to explain a few expressions of naval tactics. "Line ahead" means a line of ships steaming behind each other. When the ships steam side by side they are in "Line abreast." If they steam diagonally ahead of or behind each other they are "disposed on a line of bearing." A fleet which is cruising usually steams in line ahead, and as a rule the strongest squadron is in the van and the weakest in the rear. On such occasions the battle-cruisers take station ahead of the battleships and are generally also in line ahead. Ahead of the battle-cruisers the light cruisers are disposed as a scouting force. The rate of steaming is generally not more than fifteen to seventeen knots, though the ships have steam up in all the boilers so that they can put on full steam the moment they get news of the enemy.

Now how does a fleet, which is deploying against the enemy whose approximate position has been reported to it by its light cruisers, but whose actual position is not known, protect itself from "crossing the T"? On this matter there is one very simple rule. We must bring our own fleet up on a line at right-angles to the direction in which we suspect the centre of the hostile fleet is to be found and thus get the centre of our own line opposite the enemy's centre. We shall thus get the enemy "by his centre." With such dispositions we shall close the enemy at full speed in a broad formation. The squadrons will steam in line abreast or in short line ahead, the divisions consisting of not more than four ships. As soon as we know whether the enemy is deploying to port or starboard we shall turn our whole line on approximately the same course as that of the enemy, and by sending forward our swift battle-cruisers and steaming in line ahead at our maximum speed get across the head of the enemy's line. In this attempt to envelop or head off the hostile fleet the faster fleet will always, have a great advantage.

If, in the course of the action, the fleets get within short range—by which I mean ranges under 100 hm.—the fleet furthest ahead enjoys the further advantage that it can use its torpedoes sooner than the fleet further back. The latter is running to a certain extent *into* the torpedoes fired at it while the former is running *away* from the torpedoes fired at it from behind.

Thus a ship from the squadron ahead which possesses torpedoes of 100 hm. range can fire them when the enemy is still 120 hm. and more away, while a ship of the squadron further astern must be within 80 hm. or less in order to be able to use its torpedoes. Of course there is no question of using torpedoes except at short range, and the English, aware of the torpedo danger and the high penetrating power of our ammunition, always tried to avoid such ranges. Thanks to the higher speed the English ships of every type possessed in comparison with German ships of the same type, they were unfortunately always in a position to keep us at the distance that suited them.

To obtain the best position from the point of view of wind, sea and sun tedious manoeuvres are necessary and here again the faster fleet always has the advantage. Thus even during the Skagerrak battle the superior speed of the English enabled them to convert what was for them a bad position from the point of view of wind into a good one, which also gave them the pull from the point of view of light.

I will close this chapter, as I think I have discussed those principles of naval tactics which are necessary to a proper understanding of the mighty conflict which we called the "Battle of the Skagerrak," and the English the "Battle of Jutland."

CHAPTER 4

The Historical Value of Personal Accounts of Naval Actions

When a man sits down to recount his war experiences two methods are open to him. In the first, the narrator takes his own experiences, the details of which are often uninteresting to many of his audience or readers, and decorates them romantically with what he has heard from other sources. He even combines them, and his business is not so much to give an absolutely truthful picture of the events in which he actually participated personally as to paint a thrilling picture in lively colours of the whole action, which shall be as complete as possible. The, other method of describing war experiences is that in which the narrator confines himself strictly to speaking only of what he himself witnessed, however homely his own experience may have been or however trivial in comparison with the grandeur and immensity of the whole action. In this case the narrator is conscious in everything he says of his historical responsibility, even in the smallest details. It will be my endeavour to employ this second method in describing the Skagerrak battle.

Lowestoft had shown me very plainly that even immediately after an action it is almost impossible to reconstruct the course of events in the fight from the verbal reports of those who took part in it. It was the custom in our navy for no gunnery-logs to be kept, as every man had to devote all his energies to the action itself. Thus, immediately after the fight off Lowestoft I was not able to establish beyond dispute at what ranges and in what direction we had approximately fired when we bombarded the towns, and then fired at the cruisers and destroyers. Opinions as to whether the enemy destroyers had fled west or east were utterly conflicting when we came to draw up the report of the action!

I therefore decided that in all future actions a detailed and careful record of all orders and occurrences relating to the gunnery side as well as my own observations should be kept. I commissioned a tried senior petty officer in the transmitting station of the main armament to record each order given by me.

He heard all my orders through his head telephone, which was connected with the one by means of which I communicated with the Spotting Officer in the fore-top and the midshipman at the elevation clock in the transmitting station. In addition to my orders, for every salvo of the main armament he recorded with what elevation (*i.e.*, at what range from the enemy) it was fired and in what direction the gun was trained. The direction is given from the bow, beginning at 0. When the guns are directed from the star-board beam they are at 90°, at 180° they are pointed straight aft and at 270° on the port beam. In the transmitting station was an electric control apparatus which registered exactly the direction of each gun-turret in degrees at the given moment. Against each order and each shot the exact time within ten seconds was also recorded.

With the help of the battle charts prepared by the navigating officer during the action, and plotted with the greatest accuracy according to the compass and log by a petty officer in the transmitting station, it was easy to fix afterwards the exact position of the enemy at a given time if the direction of fire and the range at given times were known. This system of keeping a gunnery-log I introduced at firing and battle practice after the battle of Lowestoft. I also had recorded all orders and reports received at, or issued from, other important action stations, such as gun-turrets and the transmitting station for the secondary armament. In addition I had all important events recorded in the after-control, which was the action station of the Second Gunnery Officer, my deputy, and the Fourth Gunnery Officer, the deputy of the Third Gunnery Officer.

At practice I repeatedly emphasized the great value I placed on the keeping of these records in action. During the battle of Skagerrak the records were kept in all the places ordered and these put me in a position to give an exact account of almost every single shot fired. Apart from this, these records make it easy to plot a mathematically accurate chart of the action if the position of the enemy ships is fixed at those points where salvoes are known to have hit or to have fallen quite close to them. My report of the battle is based on these records, which are still in my possession, and on my diary and letters home. Unfortunately the records kept by the 30.5-cm. turrets "Caesar" and "Dora" were lost with the total destruction of these turrets. On the 9th June, 1917, an article appeared in the English journal, *The Spectator*, dealing with the value of official and personal accounts of sea fights and in particular of the Battle of Skagerrak.

The author, Bennet Copplestone, gives an excellent summing-up of the value of all such accounts as they must inevitably appear in war time when they are decisively influenced by the censor and military interests. This makes it all the more important that all those who describe their war experiences after the war should endeavour to write only what they can personally guarantee to be historically accurate. I believe the author of the article in the *Spectator* was even then making a serious effort to determine the true course of the battle from the English and German accounts. Naturally he could not completely avoid looking at the matter with English eyes. The author reveals to us some completely new facts about the battle, particularly the tactics of the leader of the English battle-cruisers, Admiral Beatty, who took advantage of the greatly superior speed of his ships to bring off a splendid out-flanking manoeuvre. I reproduce here the *Spectator* article, the publication of which in German newspapers in 1917 was prohibited by the German censor.

SEA FIGHT OFF THE SKAGERRAK.—WHAT THE GERMANS CLAIM.

Mit dem Wissen wächst der Zweifel (Doubt grows up with Knowledge).—Goethe.

It is a great mistake to dismiss German official and personal accounts of naval actions as fiction composed with intent to deceive. Even if they contained no word of truth, they would be worth study as unconscious revelations of the mind of the enemy. The German communications vary greatly in quality. Graf von Spec's letters on Coronel set forth the modest uncoloured story of a brave and honourable gentleman. Descriptions furnished by his officers of the Coronel and Falklands[1] actions are in value equal to the contemporary stories of English officers serving in those sea fights. Very few officers or men in a naval action see anything at all of what takes place; some

---

1. *The Naval War of 1914 Two Actions at Sea During the Early Phase of the First World War-The Action off Heligoland August 1914* by L. Cecil Jane and *Coronel and the Falkland Islands* by A. Neville Hilditch, also published by Leonaur.

more favourably placed see a great deal; but when one comes to examine individual accounts, even of those most favourably placed for observation, the discrepancies are baffling. The personal equation dominates all stories. Official communications, whether German or English, are the concentrated essence of a mass of individual observations cut and censored for political or military reasons. We get in the result an English distortion and a German distortion, direct conflict of evidence on observed facts, an obviously English point of view and another point of view as obviously German.

The English accounts of Jutland were written by men who were disappointed; a chance had come to them to destroy the High Seas Fleet, to cut away the base upon which the whole fabric of German naval plans rested. They were robbed of their chance by low visibility at the critical stage, and by the consummate skill with which the German Admiral Scheer made use of the mist and darkness to withdraw his outnumbered and out-manoeuvred Fleet. On the other hand, the German accounts are those of men exalted—*de têtes montées*—of men who had seen themselves and their Fleet within a very little of total destruction and had been saved as by a miracle. Their stories, both official and personal, glow with exaltation. But when the Germans call the sea fight off the Skagerrak a victory they do not mean that the English Fleet was defeated in the military sense. They mean that it was baffled of its purpose to destroy themselves. They had been in the Lion's jaws, but had managed to wriggle out before those terrible jaws could close.

That is what the Germans mean when they celebrate Skagerrak (Jutland) as a 'victory.' They declare that the battle of May 31st, 1916, 'confirmed the old truth that the large fighting ship, the ship which combines the maximum of strength in attack and defence, rules the seas.' The relation of strength, they say, between the English and German Fleets 'was roughly two to one.' They do not claim that the English superiority in strength was sensibly reduced by the losses in the battle, nor that the large English fighting ships—admittedly larger, much more numerous, and more powerfully gunned than their own—ceased after Skagerrak to rule the seas. Their claim, critically examined, is simply that, in the circumstances, it was a very successful escape for the German ships. And so indeed it was.

This sense of exultation, of almost inexpressible relief, runs through the long official story which was published in the German papers of July 1st to 5th, 1916. It is not less to be seen and felt in the glowing description of Captain Scheibe, who at the time of the action was a First Lieutenant in one of the German battle-cruisers. His '*Die Seeschlacht vor dem Skagerrak*'—of which an abridged translation was published in the *Journal* of the R.U.S.I. of February—weaves his own experiences into the Marinamt's official narrative. I have examined both these stories line by line, seeking to winnow out the grains of truth from the chaff flung about in handfuls to please the civilians of the Fatherland. In some respects these stories are quite wonderfully accurate. There is an outstanding notorious mistake, a rather curious mistake: Captain Scheibe, who was with the battle-cruisers, accepts the official statement that there were five *Queen Elizabeths* in our Fifth Battle Squadron, and that one (*Warspite*) was sunk. We know that there were but four—the *Queen Elizabeth* herself was absent and that not one was lost.

Apart from this mistake, Captain Scheibe and the official story identify and place the big ships on our side without apparent difficulty. I have never yet found a list of the five German battle-cruisers which, under Hipper, were first encountered by Beatty upon which our authorities are agreed. As against this English uncertainty—in regard to a squadron which was under observation from the first when the light was not bad—the Germans give the names and classes of our battle-cruisers and battleships with complete confidence. They are remarkably good at identifying ships which they saw; but their understanding of what they did not see is imperfect.

The Germans divide the battle into four phases in much the same manner as we do ourselves. There was, first, the encounter and the running fight between the English and German battle-cruisers, six English and five German. Up to the end of this phase, in which the *Queen Mary* and *Indefatigable* were sunk, there is no great divergence between the English and the German stories. The lamentable loss of the *Indefatigable* and the *Queen Mary* unhappily did give the Germans substantial reason for crowing. The second phase then began. Beatty turned to the north and raced away to head off the German line. The Fifth Battle Squadron, which had been too far off to take much part

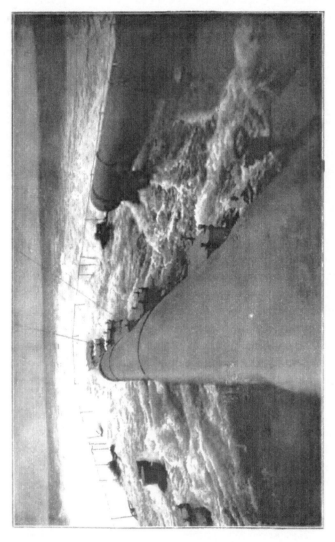

The Quarter-deck of the *Derrflinger* at Full Speed

in the first phase, remained to engage all the German battleships and battle-cruisers within range, and, by stalling off the Germans, to give Beatty's diminished squadrons the opportunity to execute a most effective manoeuvre. Here we reach a great discrepancy between the English and German stories.

We know that Beatty did in fact complete his tremendous task, did get round the head of the enemy's line, and did open up the way for Jellicoe's later deployment. The Germans dismiss Beatty and his battle-cruisers into space as no longer in the *picture* they 'were gradually disappearing in the distance, and, so far as was noticed, took no further part in the battle on account of the considerable damage they had already suffered.' This profoundly obtuse sentence occurs both in the official story and in Captain Scheibe's pamphlet, and illuminates the mental confusion of the enemy in regard to the higher tactics of the battle.

The third phase is described by the Germans as a 'battle with the whole concentrated force of the English Grand Fleet.' Visibility was poor, the mist troubled both sides, and it is difficult to make out what really happened. The Germans slur over their spiral turn towards the south—and their home ports—within the enveloping arc of the Fifth Battle Squadron, Jellicoe's Main Fleet, and Hood and Beatty's battle-cruisers; but the fact is admitted between the lines. Much is made of Scheer's decision, when confronted by greatly superior forces, to 'attack' and to keep on attacking. The claim is that the German battle-cruisers and destroyers, covering the withdrawal of the battleships, attacked twice successfully, and that when they rushed in to attack a third time the English Fleet had disappeared! 'In what direction he had fallen back before the third attack prepared for him it is impossible to determine.'

We know that Scheer did withdraw his Main Fleet in a very masterly fashion out of the closing jaws of Jellicoe. We know that he held Jellicoe off: with most gallant and spirited torpedo attacks, so that we could rarely close in to within a visible range of the German battleships. In this limited sense Scheer 'attacked'—he fought an effective rearguard action—but a retirement, covered by battle-cruisers and destroyers against superior forces, is not quite the same thing as a 'battle with the whole concentrated force of the English Grand Fleet.'

How the opposing Fleets, with their screens of light cruisers and destroyers, so completely lost touch after the night scrimmage—one cannot call it a battle—that the dawn found them out of sight of one another, I am unable to explains Neither the English nor German stories give one the slightest help. It may be presumed that the Germans made off, under cover of the darkness, for the protection of their minefields. Their own story is far otherwise. 'When the first ray of dawn reddened the eastern sky on the historic "First of June" everyone expected the rising sun to illuminate the English line drawn up for a new battle. These hopes were dashed. The horizon, all round as far as the eye could see, was empty.' One may, without injustice, dismiss the dashed 'hopes' as guff. A battle fleet which is, by its own admission, not half the strength of its opponent does not welcome the renewal of an action at dawn of a long summer day. It was very lucky indeed for the Germans that the dawn found the sea empty.

I do not propose to discuss the estimates of losses inflicted upon their respective enemies by the English and the Germans. Our own losses have been officially stated; the Germans have issued a list of theirs, and however firm one's belief may be that the German admitted losses are understated, there is no definite evidence to compel a further disclosure. Observations of damage done to an enemy during the confusion of a naval fight, especially when the light is bad, are highly untrustworthy. Damaged vessels fall out of a rapidly moving line, and are often believed to have sunk when they are making crippled for ports of safety. We shall probably never know how much damage was done by us at Jutland to the German Fleet.

Bennet Copplestone.

This article in the *Spectator* shows the difficulty of getting a clear idea of a sea-battle. In order to be able to give a perfectly accurate account of the Battle of Skagerrak, the historian must have at his disposal all the official and personal records of both sides. But the English will have no interest in giving to posterity an unvarnished account of the details of this battle, so inglorious for them. And are we to undertake this after our naval collapse and with a pacifist government at our head? I hope so! Meanwhile we who took part in the action must do our part to ensure that this duel of the "Two White Nations," sea-power against sea-power, is passed on truthfully to our posterity.

CHAPTER 5

On Board the "Derfflinger," Heading for Skagerrak

On 31st May, 1916, the battle-cruisers weighed anchor at 3 a.m. There were the *Lützow* (the flagship of Officer Commanding the reconnaissance squadron, Vice-Admiral Hipper), *Derfflinger*, *Moltke* and *Von der Tann*. We had spent the night at anchor in the Schillig Roads, off the entrance to the Jadebusen. Ahead of us stretched the small cruisers and some flotillas of destroyers. It was a beautiful, clear night which soon gave place to a splendid morning. The sun rose magnificently, covered the sea with its golden rays and soon showed us the picture of the whole High Seas Fleet proceeding to meet the enemy, always a wonderful sight and one never to be forgotten. Far ahead of us steamed the small cruisers in line ahead, surrounded by a cordon of destroyers steaming ceaselessly round the cruisers, on the look-out for enemy submarines, like dogs round a flock of sheep.

Then came the battle-cruisers. Five powerful ships with imposing names, the pride of the fleet. The *Lützow* and the *Derfflinger* of the same class, both completed during the war, the *Lützow* having only joined the fleet two months before the battle. One of the first cruises of the *Lützow* had been against Lowestoft. The *Derfflinger* and the rest of the battle-cruisers had been in action together at Scarborough and the Dogger Bank (24th January, 1915) and Lowestoft. All the battle-cruisers had been in action and were manned by picked officers and excellent ship's companies, as yet uninfected by harmful influences. On the 31st May the *Derfflinger* carried 1,398 men, practically her full complement as none was absent on leave and only quite a small number were sick. A batch of men were to have gone on leave the day before, when the order came to get ready to put to sea, so we kept them back. The fact that no man happened to be absent on leave helped greatly towards securing complete co-operation in action.

The captain of the *Derfflinger* was Captain Hartog, the second-in-command, Commander Fischer (Max), navigating officer, Commander von Jork. The gunnery officers under me were: Second Gunnery Officer, Lieutenant-Commander Lamprecht; Third Gunnery Officer, Lieutenant-Commander Hausser; Fourth Gunnery Officer, Lieutenant-Commander von Mellenthin; turret-officers, Lieutenant-Commander Freiherr v. Speth-Schulzburg, Lieutenants, Hankow and von Boltenstern; the observation officers, Lieutenant von Stosch and Lieutenant Schulz; communications officer, Lieutenant Hoch, and Bg. officer, Lieutenant Friedrich. The torpedo officers were: Lieutenant-Commander Kossak, Lieutenants Schilling and von der Decken. Adjutant and signal-officer, Lieutenant Peters. Wireless officer, Lieutenant Thaer. Medical officer, Staff-Surgeon Dr. Freyer. Chief engineer, Engineer-Commander Kohn. All officers with the exception of Lieutenant-Commander von Mellenthin, who was doing a course, were on board.

The battle-cruisers, too, were surrounded by a cordon of destroyers which circled round us like a swarm of excited insects. On our numerous cruises in the North Sea and the Baltic, we had often drawn the torpedo fire of English submarines, but so far the only successful shot had been one that hit the *Moltke*. During the attack on Lowestoft the *Seidlitz* had struck a mine, and had been forced to turn back damaged after the Admiral had transferred his flag to the *Lützow*. It was necessary therefore to keep a sharp lookout if all five of us were to reach the Norwegian coast, for which we were said to be making.

Far astern the clear weather enabled us to see the main fleet, our ships of the line. These numbered twenty-two, a proud armada. They were led by the 3rd Squadron, our most modern ships, with the flagship, the *König*, ahead, then the Fleet-flagship, the *Friedrich der Grosse*, flying the flag of the commander-in-chief, Admiral Scheer. Then the 1st Squadron, the ships of the *Heligoland* and *Nassau* class, and finally the 2nd Squadron, the obsolescent battleships of the Deutschland class, including my old ship the *Hessen*, on which I had for five years directed so much firing-practice as gunnery officer.

The ships of the line were surrounded by a considerable number of light cruisers, which served as a screen for both flanks of the fleet. In addition to these there was, of course, the usual swarm of destroyers scouting for submarines and mines. We steered west of Heligoland and the Amrum bank on a northerly course. One half of the gun-crews were manning the guns, the other half were sleeping in their hammocks slung near the guns or near their respective action stations, such as ammunition chambers, transmitting stations, etc. I spent the night on the bridge. While cruising I had no definite duties to perform. The Second and Third Gunnery Officers shared the watch. My Commanding Officer laid down the principle that the first officer, the First Gunnery Officer and the First Torpedo Officer should get as much sleep and rest as possible, so that they might be fresh when the ship came into action. An excellent principle which with us was followed not only in theory but in practice.

For me, therefore, every cruise of this kind was a complete rest. If there was news of the enemy, or if there was anything unusual to be seen, or in particularly fine weather, of course I kept to the bridge. For the rest, however, I slept, read, or played chess in the ward-room and made a round of all the guns only about once every two hours, talked with the officers and gun-layers on watch and saw that everything was in order. As a rule "The Goblin" came with me on my rounds through the ship and we frequently came across something that had to be put right immediately. "The Goblin" called his band together, the electrical artificers, armourers, the transmitting-station specialists, and in a very short time I received the message: "Port elevation telegraph third 15-cm. gun in working order again!" "Left gun-mounting in Caesar turret repaired!" and so on.

Of course I was always on the bridge when we came to an area where submarines or mines had been recently reported, and on dark nights when destroyer attacks might be expected. But I could make my own arrangements, and so these days of cruising were generally a very pleasant time for me.

I had a large double cabin on the upper deck, not too near the ship's side. Consequently I could keep my scuttle open except in rough weather. In this way I had from my cabin a good view of the sea and saw at once if anything unusual was happening.

After enjoying the sunrise on the 31st May—a sight which at sea was a never-failing source of joy, though at anchor in the brown *Jade-wasser*, it could not drag me out of my bunk—I lay down again for another couple of hours' sleep, after which I appeared, shaved, washed and rested, for breakfast in the mess. Most of the officers had to forego the luxury of a careful *toilette*, as they couldn't get to their cabins between decks owing to the fact that all the hatches had been battened down and watertight doors closed as a precaution against mines. After breakfast I sat down in my comfortable cabin, dealt with some writing work and enjoyed the view over the sea. Before midday dinner a round of the guns and then dinner, at which the natural subject of conversation was: shall we see the enemy? The goal of our cruise was further afield than had so far been the case. On the night of the 1st June, the cruisers and destroyers were to search for enemy and neutral merchantmen off the Skagerrak. It was to be supposed that on this night our presence off the Skagerrak would be made known, that the English fleet would put to sea from England with all possible speed and that there was even a chance of encountering the English Grand Fleet on the 1st June.

Moreover, strong forces of English armoured cruisers and light cruisers had been reported in the neighbourhood of the Norwegian coast, and an encounter with these was probable for the 1st June, and was not out of the question for the 31st May. That the entire English fleet was already at sea and bearing on the same point as ourselves, not a man in the German fleet suspected, not even the commander-in-chief. And in the same way, according to all published reports, no one in the English fleet knew that the German fleet had put to sea. There is no reason to believe that this was not the case, and yet in the inland parts of the country the question is always being asked: How did the English get to know that we were off the Skagerrak? Or: How did we learn that the English intended to enter the Baltic?

All such talk is mere idle chatter. As has been stated by both Admiralties, the battle of the Skagerrak came about by an accidental meeting of the two fleets on one of their many cruises in the North Sea. When it is considered that the North Sea is larger than Germany, and how easy it is in such a large area for two cruising fleets to pass one another unnoticed, there can be nothing but wonder at the strange chance that brought the head of their scouting squadron right on to that of the English. The Battle of Jutland[1] developed in the early stages like a carefully prepared instructional manoeuvre, in which, according to plan, first the light cruisers, then the battle cruisers, and finally the ships of the line come into action.

At midday dinner, at which the officers of the watch were not present, there was great excitement and enthusiasm. Nearly everyone was agreed that this time there would be an action, but no one spoke

---

1. *The Fighting at Jutland* by H. W. Fawcett & G. W. W. Hooper, also published by Leonaur.

LINE AHEAD.

LINE OF BEARING.

of anything more important than an action involving the lighter fighting forces or the older armoured cruisers. No one thought of the possibility that the whole English Fleet could be only a few hours away from us. Some few were pessimistic, and said we should soon turn about again without having accomplished anything. The P.M.O. always carried a large pocket compass about with him, which he used to place beside him on the table, for, as the ward-room scuttles were closed, and consequently the sea could not be seen, we could not tell when the ship altered course. We used to call him our between-deck strategist. He now kept a careful eye on his compass.

Altogether there was a tense atmosphere about the mess, as though we were on the eve of important happenings. As was always the case when we were engaged in one of our sweeps of the North Sea, no one drank a drop of alcohol at meals, and that, in spite of the fact that we were none of us despisers of wine, woman and song. On all cruises in war-time we treated ourselves like sportsmen in training: from the moment of putting to sea until we came back to our home moorings we were practically all total abstainers.

We smoked our cigars, and then the junior officers took the watch while those they had relieved came down to dinner. I went to my cabin, lay down for a *siesta*, watched the blue rings from my cigar, and dreamed of battle and victory. If only it came to gunnery action this time! My whole career seemed so incomplete, so much of a failure if I did not have at least one opportunity of feeling in battle on the high seas what fighting was really like. Blow for blow, shot for shot, that was what I wanted. I had had twelve years' experience of gunnery practice; I had learned all about it. It was a sport I understood. Once I had fixed the target with the periscope and once the first salvo had crashed from the guns, nothing could disturb me. It is true I did not yet know how I should get on in the dense hail of enemy fire. But that did not worry me. I should find that out all in good time.

At two o'clock the drums beat through the ship. A long roll. The signal to clean guns. Every man except the officers had to go to his action station. For the gunnery officer this is the most important hour of the day. At gun-cleaning all the machinery is set in motion, cleaned, oiled; all apparatus carefully adjusted. I went from gun to gun, accompanied by "The Goblin." In the "Bertha" turret the fore-most rope of the ammunition hoist had given way, and in replacing this it was discovered that the wire rope was badly perished in one place. I decided that it should be replaced by a new rope. This took about an hour. For an hour the enemy would, if possible, have to oblige us by keeping away! I made sure that the gun crews were provided with all they needed for action.

On the 29th May the fleet had at last, after prolonged pressure, been provided with a few thousand gas-masks from the army. The commander-in-chief had given orders that these should be issued to the battle-cruisers and the most modern ships of the line. Now we had to see that every man had his gas-mask at hand near his action station. In the gun turrets the ammunition for immediate use lay near the guns, everywhere in the small quantity stipulated by regulations. The guns of the secondary armament were already loaded, so as to be able to open fire at once at any submarine that might chance to break surface.

For the time between three and four o'clock, the Commander, who regulates the division of duty on board, had placed the gun crews at my disposal, and I had started some gun drill and turret exercises. My officers and men were not too pleased with this, but I knew only too well how great my responsibility was. I could only answer for the perfect working of the whole complicated apparatus if each part of it were set moving once more under battle conditions. The Third Gunnery Officer, who controlled the secondary armament, came with me somewhat reluctantly to the fore-control for the fire-control practice. We fixed our telephone receivers over our heads and got to work. "Normal direction for starboard fire!" In the transmitting-stations about forty levers were moved as directed. All parts of the ship received the order: "Direction for starboard fire!"

I had trained my periscope on one of our small cruisers and gave the order: "Direction indicated!" All the other gunnery periscopes and all the guns were trained on the electric indicators, and so with absolute accuracy on the given target fixed by my sighting petty officer. I called: "Question: E-U?" This meant: The Gunnery Observation Officer will report at once to the First Gunnery Officer what is the rate of change of range per minute, minus or plus, shown by his E-U range indicator. And the Bg. Officer will report the change of range per minute calculated from the difference of the range-finder readings. "Report from the fore-top: the new E-U range indicator is missing in the fore-top!" "Good God! the thing must be fetched at once from the gunnery office. Gunner's mate X will report to me after duty. The fore-top meanwhile will carry on with the old indicator!"

I should like to say a few words here about E-U (*Entfernungs-Un-*

73

terschieds) indicator. It was invented in its newest form by Commander Paschen, the First Gunnery Officer of the *Lützow*. It served at the same time to determine the range variation (E-U), and to fix the deflection. I will not bother the reader here with a description of the fixing of the deflection; it is enough for him to know that to compensate for all influences which may deviate the shot laterally from its true course, a lateral correction is effected by what is called a deflection-corrector. The influences which may deviate the shot laterally from its original line are: wind, the ship's speed and the rifling of the gun.

A further correction must be made to take into account the enemy's speed. The excellent, highly-perfected apparatus invented by Commander Paschen allowed the deflection to be read off without any calculation after the estimated speed and course of the enemy had been determined; the gunnery officer himself had only to correct further for the wind. The principal object of the E-U indicator was to determine the range variation per minute or "rate." The apparatus was first adjusted to the ship's speed, all variations of which were reported from the fore-control. The enemy's speed and course were then estimated, and a further adjustment made.

The range variation could then be read off the indicator without any further calculation. This apparatus had already been fitted all over the ship, for the most part, it is true, of an older type, which did not allow of reading off the deflection. If the fore-top was put out of action, the gunnery officer could have the range variation calculated in another part of the ship, even though the man at the indicator could not see the enemy. Of course, the gunnery officer would then have to keep him posted during the action with all information as to course and speed, which would make the fire-control very difficult. In addition to this, the gunnery officers themselves were supplied with similar apparatus, so that in action they could check the reports of the observation officers, and could themselves estimate the range variation, in case communication with the observation officers should be interrupted.

The fire-control practice continued: "15,000! Salvoes fire!" The orders were passed from the transmitting-station to the 30.5-cm. turrets by telephone and fire-gong. On the order, "Fire!"—during rapid fire the moment the gun was fired—the men whose duty it was to announce the fall of shot, and who were stationed behind the communications officers in the fore-top, gun-positions and fire-controls, immediately pressed back the levers of the hit-indicators. Then came a tense silence. At the end of the time corresponding to the trajectory, each hit-indicator should emit a loud buzz, which can only be compared to the bleating of a flock of sheep.

With my telephone receiver I ought to have heard simultaneously the buzz of the hit-indicators of the heavy guns from the fore-top, the fore-control and the transmitting-station. But I only heard one, that of the fore-top. "Question: Why are the hit-indicators not being used?" "Report: Hit-indicators have been used but are not working!" More work for "The Goblin." I order: "Fresh elements to be put at once in all hit-indicators!" and so it goes on, until at last I am convinced that all defects are made good, and that the guns are completely ready for action. With this pleasant feeling I return to the wardroom to enjoy an excellent cup of coffee on the comfortable leather settee.

I could have done with a considerably longer period in this position, but at 4.28 the alarm bells rang through the ship, both drums beat for action, and the boatswains of the watch piped and shouted: "Clear for action!"

CHAPTER 6

First Phase of the Battle
of Skagerrak (5.48 to 6.55 p.m.)

When I reached the bridge a report had come through from the *Frankfort* saying that isolated enemy forces had been sighted to the westward. The battle-cruisers were already steaming in line ahead at full speed towards the reported position. Ahead of us could be seen the light cruisers, with their destroyers driving forward amid dense clouds of smoke. Our own main fleet was no longer in sight. Our escorting destroyers could scarcely keep up with us; they lost much weigh owing to the heavy swell. Otherwise, however, the sea was fairly smooth, with only a light north-westerly wind, wind pressure 3.

I climbed up to the fore-control. I say climbed, as a considerable climb was necessary after passing through the armoured door to reach the platform on which the gunnery periscopes stood. Already reports were coming in: "Secondary armament clear!" "Order communication clear!" "Fore-top, after control, main-top clear," and so on. Finally all gun positions had reported, and I reported to the captain: "Guns clear."

We officers adjusted our head-telephones and were ready for the show to begin. I now ask the reader to study closely the accompanying sketch. The first time indicated is 4.28 p.m. Until then the battle-cruisers had been steering a northerly course. At 4.28 they swung round on a westerly course, which was maintained until 5.22. After that the courses steered were north until 5.33, south until 6.53, north until 7.55, widely varied courses until 9.20, west until 9.45, and then mainly south until the end of the day's fighting. With the help of this sketch it will be easy for the reader to follow in my description of the individual phases of the battle the course of the *Derfflinger*, which was at the same time the course of the rest of the battle-cruisers and of the enemy's ships which were engaged by the *Derfflinger*. The red dotted lines running from the *Derfflinger's* course show the direction and range (in hm.) of the salvoes which were registered in the gunnery log as hits, or at any rate as straddling the enemy. In the case of these salvoes the range given is the true range, so that the end of the range line is at the same time the position of the enemy at the moment of impact.

The course of the enemy engaged is indicated by a red line. This course is mathematically correct in so far as it is established by the range of our salvoes. The course between these points cannot claim to be mathematically accurate, but cannot be far out from the actual course of the English ships.

We steered, therefore, to begin with, about half an hour west and then half an hour north-west.

All our periscopes and telescopes were trained on the enemy, but the smoke from our light cruisers hampered our view. About five o' clock we heard the first shots, and soon saw that the *Elbing* was being engaged and was returning the fire strongly. My log-keeper in the transmitting-station wrote under the first report I sent to the guns: "*5.5.* Our light cruisers report four enemy light cruisers! Nothing yet visible from the *Derfflinger!*" And later the following orders:

5.30. Our light cruisers have opened fire! Direction on the second cruiser from the right! Load with high-explosive shell and fix safety bolt! Train on extreme right water-line! 18,000! Fire from the right! Deflection left 20! 17,000!

It was already beginning to get hot in the fore-control, so I took off my overcoat and had it hung in the chart-room behind. I never saw it again!

At this time none of us yet realized that we were engaging enemy ships of our own type. Then a message from the captain reached me in the fore-control: "Enemy battle-cruisers have been reported," I passed this message on to the gun crews. It was now clear that within a short time a life-and-death struggle would develop For a moment there was a marked hush in the fore-control. But this only lasted a minute or so, then humour broke out again, and everything went on in perfect order and calm. I had the guns trained on what would be approximately the enemy's position. I adjusted my periscope to its extreme power—fifteen diameters, the adjustment for perfect visibility. But still there was no sign of the enemy. Nevertheless, we could see a change in the situation: the light cruisers and destroyers had turned about and were taking shelter behind the battle-cruisers. Thus we were at the head of the line. The horizon ahead of us grew clear of smoke, and we could now make out some English light cruisers which had also turned about.

Suddenly my periscope revealed some big ships. Black monsters; six tall, broad-beamed giants steaming in two columns. They were still a long way off, but they showed up clearly on the horizon, and even at this great distance they looked powerful, massive. We only maintained our northerly course a short time longer. At 5.33 our flagship *Lützow*, immediately astern of which we were following as second in the line, swung round on a southerly course. The enemy also altered to a southerly converging course, and so both lines steamed south at full speed, coming continually nearer together. Admiral Hipper's intention was clear: he meant to engage the enemy battle-cruisers and draw them on to our main fleet.

The log-keeper at this time entered my orders:

*5.35.*Ship turning to starboard! Normal direction for starboard fire! 17,000! 16,500! Heavy guns armour-piercing shell! Direction on second battle-cruiser from the right, 102 degrees! Ship making 26 knots, course E.S.E.! 17,000! Our target has two masts and two funnels, as well as a narrow funnel close to the foremast! Deflection 19 left! Rate 100 minus! 16,400!

Still no permission to open fire from the flagship!

It became clear that both sides were trying for a decision at medium range. Meanwhile I examined the enemy carefully. The six giants recalled to my mind the day on which I had gone out to meet the English squadron in the Kiel Bight to welcome the English admiral. Once more I saw the proud English squadron approaching, but this time the welcome would be very different! How much bigger and more menacing the enemy ships appeared this time, magnified fifteen times! I could now recognize them as the six most modern enemy battle-cruisers. Six battle-cruisers were opposed to our five: we went into the battle with nearly equal forces. It was a stimulating, majestic spectacle as the dark-grey giants approached like fate itself.

The six ships, which had at first been proceeding in two columns, formed line ahead. Like a herd of prehistoric monsters they closed on one another with slow movements, spectre-like, irresistible.

THE SECONDARY ARMAMEMT FIRING A SALVO

But now there were other things to be done than gaze at the enemy. The measured ranges were continually decreasing. When we got to 165 hm. I had given the order: "Armour-piercing shell!" That was the projectile for close-range fighting. Now every man in the ship knew that it was to be a short-range struggle, for I had often explained how the two types of projectile were to be used.

Following the reports of the Bg. officer, I gave the ranges continually to the guns. Immediately after altering course the signal was hoisted on the flagship: "Take targets from the left!" That meant that each German ship was to train on a corresponding English ship, reckoning from the left. Accordingly the first five English ships were to be engaged by our five German battle-cruisers, and to the *Derfflinger* fell the second ship in the line, which I identified as of the *Queen Mary* class. It was the *Princess Royal*, a sister-ship of the *Queen Mary*. All was ready to open fire, the tension increased every second, but I could not yet give the first order to fire. I had to wait for the signal from the flagship: "Open fire." Our enemy, too, were still holding their fire and coming continually closer.

"15,000!" As my last order rang out there was a dull roar. I looked ahead. The *Lützow* is firing her first salvo and immediately the signal "Open fire" is hoisted. In the same second I shout: "Salvoes-fire!" and like thunder our first salvo crashes out. The ships astern follow suit at once and we see all round the enemy jets of fire and rolling clouds of smoke—the battle has begun! My log-keeper in the transmitting station wrote at 5.48: "5.48. Ship turning to starboard! Rate 200 closing! 15,000! Salvoes-fire!" Nearly thirty seconds pass before our hit-recorders—this time all three together—"bleat." The newly-adjusted elements have saved the situation! The splashes are well together, but "over," *i.e.*, behind the target and to the right. "Deflection 2 more left! down 400! continue!"

Those were the orders for the next salvo. "Down 400!": the midshipman in charge of the elevation telegraph had to put back the indicator 400 m. And "continue" meant: as soon as he had made his adjustments he was himself to give from the transmitting station the order "salvoes-fire!" This relieved the gunnery officer; otherwise it might happen that the order "Fire" would be given before the gun was adjusted to the new elevation. The midshipman in the transmitting station could, by means of a special electric control-indicator, see that every gun was already correctly adjusted.

At the elevation telegraph in the transmitting station sat Midshipman Stachow, a young fellow of seventeen, who had charge of the elevation telegraph and the elevation clock, transmitted my orders to the gun turrets and regulated the fire orders. He was connected up to me by a head-telephone so that I could check all orders given by him. Until the end of the action this young mid-shipman regulated the fire discipline of the heavy and secondary armament coolly and efficiently—he only made one mistake and that at the beginning of the action.

The second salvo crashed out. Again it was "over." "Down 400," I ordered. The third and fourth salvoes were also over in spite of the fact that after the third I had given the order, "Down 800." "Good God, Stachow! there's something wrong," I cursed. "Down 800!" It appeared later from the gunnery-log that the midshipman had probably not understood the first "down 800," or, at any rate, it had not been acted upon. This time, however, the "down 800" was effective. The sixth salvo, fired at 5.52, straddled, three splashes over the target, one short! We had meanwhile reached a range of 11,900, as the elevation clock had shown a rate of 200 closing and then 300 closing per minute, and I had already gone down 1,600. We had already been in action four minutes and only now had we straddled our target. That wasn't a very cheering result.

Our first rounds had been well over. This was due to inaccurate estimation of the opening range and a delay in the first reports of the measured range. I explain the serious error of calculation as follows: The Bg. men were completely overwhelmed by the first view of the enemy monsters. Each one saw the enemy ship magnified twenty-three times in his instrument! Their minds were at first concentrated on the appearance of the enemy. They tried to ascertain who their enemy was. And so when the order suddenly came to open fire they had not accurately fixed the estimated range. It cannot be put down to incapacity, for throughout the remainder of the action the range-takers did their work excellently. Nor can it be put down to the inefficiency of our instruments; on the contrary our Zeiss stereoscopic finders worked admirably throughout the action. The Bg. officer reported to me later that there was seldom a variation of more than 300 m. between any of the range-finders even at the longest ranges.

Valuable minutes had been lost, but now I had found the target and at 5h. 52m. 20s. p.m. the log-keeper recorded my order: "*Gut schnell Wirkung.*" "*Gut schnell*" meant that Midshipman Stachow in the transmitting station was to give the order "Salvoes-fire!" to the heavy guns once every 20 seconds. And the word "*Wirkung*" meant that after each salvo of the heavy guns the secondary armament was to fire two salvoes in quick succession and henceforward fire in conjunction with the heavy guns. Then began an ear-splitting, stupefying din. Including the secondary armament we were firing on an average one mighty salvo every seven seconds. Anyone who has had experience of gun-fire with full charges on board a large battleship will imagine what that meant. While the firing was going on any observation was out of the question. Dense masses of smoke accumulated round the muzzles of the guns, growing into clouds as high as houses, which stood for seconds in front of us like an impenetrable wall and were then driven by the wind and the weigh over the ship.

In this way we often could see nothing of the enemy for seconds at a time as our fore-control was completely enveloped in thick smoke. Naturally such furious rapid fire could only be maintained for a limited time. It made almost superhuman demands on the gun-crews and ammunition men. Also it would be easy in time to confuse the respective splashes of the heavy and secondary armaments. I gave the order: "Secondary armament, cease fire." It was not long before our shots fell over or short, as a result of the enemy's altering course, and then the fire slackened again. Each salvo was then directed afresh and this continued until the target was again straddled. And then the devil's concert began again on the order: "Good, Rapid." Once more a salvo from the heavy guns crashed out every 20 seconds, with the secondary armament firing in the intervals. Unfortunately at that time the secondary armament could only fire at a range of 13,000 m.

What astonished me was that so far we had apparently not been hit once. Only quite rarely did a shot stray near us. I observed the gun-turrets of our target more closely and established that this ship was not firing at us. She too was firing at our flagship. I observed the third enemy ship for a moment; by some mistake we were being left out. I laughed grimly and now I began to engage our enemy with complete calm, as at gun practice, and with continually increasing accuracy. All thought of death or sinking vanished. The true sporting joy of battle awoke in me and all my thoughts concentrated on the one desire: to hit, to hit rapidly and true, to go on hitting and to damage the proud enemy in any possible way or place. He should not find it easy to bar my return to my home and hearth!

I had spoken the words, "They are not firing at us," quite gently and half to myself, but in a second the words flew from mouth to mouth in the fore-control and filled every man with unalloyed de-light. Apart from us two gunnery officers, only the two sight-setting petty officers and the Bg. officer could see anything of the enemy. It is true we had left the apertures open—from a not quite justifiable curiosity—but of course the enemy was hardly visible to the naked eye. The hands in the fore-control therefore eagerly absorbed all the information we let fall.

And now the battle continued. Our shots raised waterspouts from 80 to 100 metres high, twice as high as the enemy's masts. Our joy at being immune from fire was short-lived. The other side had noticed the mistake, and now we were often straddled by salvoes.

I again fixed the enemy gun-turrets with my periscope and watched them carefully. I now saw that they were directly trained on us. I made a further discovery which astonished me. With each salvo fired by the enemy I was able to see distinctly four or five shells coming through the air. They looked like elongated black spots. Gradually they grew bigger, and then—*crash!* they were here. They exploded on striking the water or the ship with a terrific roar.

After a bit I could tell from watching the shells fairly accurately whether they would fall short or over, or whether they would do us the honour of a visit. The shots that hit the water raised colossal splashes. Some of these columns of water were of a poisonous yellow-green tinge from the base to about half their height; these would be lyddite shells.

The columns stood up for quite five to ten seconds before they completely collapsed again. They were giant fountains, beside which the famous fountains of Versailles were mere children's toys. In a later stage of the battle, when the enemy had got our range better, it fre-quently occurred that these water-spouts broke over the ship, swamp-ing everything, but at the same time putting out any fires. The first hit that I observed struck us just over the casemate. It first pierced a door with a round glass window, behind which an excellent petty officer, Boatswain's Mate Lorenzen, had taken shelter to watch the battle. His curiosity was severely punished, the shot severing his head clean from his body.

Our distance from the enemy decreased to 11,300 m. At 5.55 p.m., however, I was again firing at an elevation of 11,500, and then the range increased further. At 5.57 I had an increase of "plus 600" re-corded on the elevation-clock. At 6 p.m. the range was 15,200; at 6.5, 18,000, our longest range. I could increase our range a little by making the gunlayers train, not on the waterline of the enemy, but on the top of the funnels, the tops and, finally, the mastheads. But that only made a difference of a few hundred metres. Subsequent to the Battle of Skagerrak, our range was increased considerably, as the result of all kinds of improvements. Now, however, we were powerless against the enemy, and could no longer return his fire. This state of affairs lasted until 6.17 p.m.

At 6.10 p.m. our flagship had turned several points to starboard; the enemy had apparently also altered course, and so we were converging on one another fairly rapidly. At 6.19 p.m. the range had already been reduced to 16,000 m.; 16 km. is indeed a very respectable range, but actually the good visibility and spotting conditions made it appear small.

The Zeiss lenses of our periscopes were excellent. At the longest distances I could make out all details of the enemy ships, as, for instance, all movements of the turrets and individual guns, which were lowered almost to the horizontal for loading. Before the war no man in our navy had thought it possible to fight effectively at a range of over 150 hm. I can still remember quite well various war games we used to play at the Kiel Casino a year or two before the war under Admiral von Ingenohl's direction, in which on principle all shooting at more than 100 hm. was ruled out as ineffective.

What was the enemy's situation now? At 6 p.m. his rear ship, the *Indefatigable*, blew up. I did not see this, as my attention was completely occupied in directing the shooting against the second ship. The sound of what must have been a terrific explosion was completely drowned by the hellish din in our own ship and the bursting of the shells round us, though when our own guns were silent we could hear the dull roar of the enemy salvoes.

In the after fire-control the blowing up of the *Indefatigable* was observed and recorded. The *Indefatigable* was engaged by our rearmost ship, the *Von der Tann*, and was sunk by excellent shooting. The successful director of the shooting on the *Von der Tann* was that ship's First Gunnery Officer, Commander Mahrholz.

The north-westerly wind was blowing the smoke from the English guns between them and us. As a result of this, their view was often hampered and shooting made difficult. As the visibility facing east was also inferior to that facing west, the English battle-cruisers had a decidedly unfavourable tactical position. The clouds of smoke in front of the enemy hampered us little, as it sufficed for our stereoscopic range-finders if the range officer could see the smallest speck of the mast-heads.

At 6.17 I again engaged the second battle-cruiser from the left. I was under the impression that it was the same ship that I had engaged before, the *Princess Royal*. Actually, however, it was the *Queen Mary*, the third ship of the enemy line. This was due to the fact that, just as I was finding my target, Admiral Beatty's flagship, the *Lion*, was obliged to fall out of the enemy line for a time, and, owing to the heavy smoke covering the enemy line, could not be seen by us. It appears from subsequent reports in the English Press that at that time Beatty transferred his flag from the *Lion*, whose conning-tower had been put out of action, to the *Princess Royal*.

Later in the battle Admiral Hipper had also to change his flagship. Our flagship, the *Lützow*, had kept the *Lion* under continuous, powerful and effective fire of high-explosive shell. The *Lutzow's* gunnery officer had preferred not to change his type of shell, as this is liable to result in certain unfavourable ballistic influences, and to fire nothing but high-explosive shell from the first. By their tremendous explosive and incendiary properties he had forced the *Lion* to leave the line for a time to extinguish fires that had broken out on board. From 6.17, therefore, I was engaging the *Queen Mary*. Certain difficulties in the fire-control now occurred, as a result of the dense smoke from the guns and funnels, which continually blurred the lenses of the periscopes over the deck of the fore-control, making it almost impossible to see anything.

When this occurred I was entirely dependent on the observations of the spotting officer in the fore-top, Lieutenant-Commander von Stosch. This excellent officer observed and reported the fall of shot with astonishing coolness, and by his admirable observation, on the correctness of which I had to rely absolutely, he contributed very considerably to the success of our gunfire. While we could see nothing, Lieutenant-Commander von Stosch, in his draughty observation post, 35 metres above sea-level, kept his fore-top periscope trained dead on the enemy. A control-indicator marked on my periscope the line of the fore-top periscope. My direction petty officer covered this with his indicator, and in this way we kept all our guns trained on the enemy without being able to see him.

Of course this was only a makeshift. Midshipman Bartel, who assisted me in the fore-control during the action, by calling out the mean ranges, working my rate and deflection indicator, and observing the enemy through the aperture, quickly remedied the defect by wiping the smoke from the lenses with mops kept specially for this purpose.

In the later phases of the battle, when from time to time the columns of water raised by the enemy fire broke over the ship and the smoke continually drove down on to the lenses, he had to clean them after nearly every shot. At last, however, the mops became too dirty, and I was reluctantly forced to send a man frequently on to the roof of the fore-control to keep the lenses clean. In this position he was unprotected from the enemy fire. This duty was carried out for the most part by my messenger from the gunnery department, Artificer Meyer, who, throughout the battle, remained on the forebridge near the fore-control, until at last fate overtook him and a splinter smashed his leg below the knee.

As I have already pointed out, from 6.10 p.m. the two lines were steering a sharply converging southerly course. At 6.15 p.m. we observed that the enemy was sending his destroyers to the attack. A little later our destroyers and the light cruiser *Regensburg* passed through our line and pressed home an attack. Between the lines of fighting battle-cruisers a small independent action developed. Here about twenty-five English destroyers and almost as many of ours waged a stubborn action and successfully prevented each other respectively from using torpedoes against the battle-cruisers. About 6.30 p.m. several torpedoes were fired against the lines on both sides, but no hit was made. This destroyer action was a magnificent spectacle for us.

During the destroyer action the two lines were continually converging, and now came what was, from the point of view of gunnery, the most interesting struggle of the day. I established that the *Queen Mary* had selected the *Derfflinger* as her target. The *Queen Mary* was firing less rapidly than we, but usually full salvoes. As she had an armament of eight 13.5-inch guns this meant that she was mostly firing eight of these powerful "*coffers,*" as the Russians called the heaviest guns during the Russo-Japanese war, against us at the same time! I could see the shells coming and I had to admit that the enemy were shooting superbly. As a rule all eight shots fell together. But they were almost always over or short—only twice did the *Derfflinger* come under this infernal hail, and each time only one heavy shell hit her.

We were firing as at gunnery practice. The head-telephones were working splendidly, and each of my orders was correctly understood. Lieutenant-Commander von Stosch reported the exact fall of each

86

shot with deadly accuracy. "Straddling! Two hits!" "Straddling! The whole salvo in the ship!"

I was trying to get in two salvoes to the enemy's one. Several times I was unable to attain this, as for full salvoes the enemy was firing with fabulous rapidity. I observed that the gunnery officer of the *Queen Mary* was firing the guns himself with central fire-control, using the famous Percy Scott "Firing-director," for all the guns fired, and the shots fell absolutely simultaneously. The English gunnery officer was probably stationed in the fore-top, where he was above the smoke, and firing the guns electrically from there. The ability to do this gave the English ships a great advantage.

Unfortunately for us it was only in the light of our experiences in this battle that we succeeded in inventing an apparatus allowing of director firing from the fore-top. I myself played not a small part in the introduction of the director firing into our navy, and conducted in the *Derfflinger* the first director firing in our fleet by a system invented by me and later generally known as the "*Derfflinger* system."

And so the *Queen Mary* and the *Derfflinger* fought out a regular gunnery duel over the destroyer action that was raging between us. But the poor *Queen Mary* was having a bad time. In addition to the *Derfflinger* she was being engaged by the *Seydlitz!* and the gunnery officer of the *Seydlitz*, Lieutenant-Commander Foerster, was our crack gunnery expert, tried in all the previous engagements in which the ship had taken part, cool-headed and of quick decision.

The *Seydlitz* only carried 28-cm. guns. These could not pierce the thickest armour of the *Queen Mary*, but every ship has less heavily armoured places which can be pierced with great damage even by a 28-cm. shell.

The good functioning of our hit-indicators prevented any danger of Lieutenant-Commander von Stosch or myself ever confusing our own shots with those from the *Seydlitz's* 28-cm. guns. As the range was always more than 130 hm. neither ship could yet bring her 15-cm. guns to bear.

A simultaneous engagement of the same enemy by two ships was also only possible so long as both ships were using their heavy guns only. If the 15-cm. guns had fired in between, it would have been impossible to distinguish the fall of the shots.

For the time between 6.22 and 6h. 26m. 10s p.m. my log-keeper in the transmitting station made out the following table:

Time, h. m. s.	Training angle.	Range in m.	Deflection.	Orders for elevation telegraph, etc.
6 22 –	52°	14,000	left 10	E-U-3 !
6 22 40	51°	13,900	,, 16	2 short !
6 23 45	52°	13,700	,, 14	1 short !
6 24 20	52°	13,500	,, 14	Good, Rapid !
6 24 40	52°	13,400	,, 14	
6 25 –	52°	13,400	,, 14	
6 25 20	52°	13,200	,, 14	
6 25 45	52°	13,100	,, 14	
6 26 10	52°	13,200	,, 10	2 short ! Heavy explosion on our enemy ! Change of target left to the second battle-cruiser from the left !

It is noticeable in this list that the training angle of the turrets remained practically unchanged and that, therefore, during these vital
minutes the ship steered an admirable course.

About 6.26 p.m. was the historic moment when the *Queen Mary*,
the proudest ship of the English fleet, met her doom. Since 6.24 p.m.
every one of our salvoes had straddled the enemy. When the salvo
fired at 6h. 26m. 10s. fell, heavy explosions had already begun in the
Queen Mary. First of all a vivid red flame shot up from her forepart.
Then came an explosion forward which was followed by a much
heavier explosion amidships, black debris of the ship flew into the air,
and immediately afterwards the whole ship blew up with a terrific
explosion.

A gigantic cloud of smoke rose, the masts collapsed inwards, the
smoke-cloud hid everything and rose higher and higher. Finally nothing but a thick, black cloud of smoke remained where the ship had
been. At its base the smoke column only covered a small area, but it
widened towards the summit and looked like a monstrous black pine.
I estimated the height of the smoke column at from 300 to 400 m.

In *The Times* of 9th June, 1916, a gunlayer of the *Tiger*, the next

BATTLESHIP FIRING.

SPLASHES MADE BY HEAVY GUNS.

astern of the *Queen Mary*, gives the following description of the sinking of the *Queen Mary*:

> The German squadron again came ahead, their guns being concentrated on the *Queen Mary*. They had been poking about for the range for some minutes without effect, when suddenly a most remarkable thing happened.
>
> Every shell that the Germans threw seemed suddenly to strike the battle-cruiser at once. It was as if a whirl-wind was smashing a forest down, and reminded me very much of the rending that is heard when a big vessel is launched and the stays are being smashed.
>
> The *Queen Mary* seemed to roll slowly to starboard, her masts and funnels gone, and with a huge hole in her side. She listed again, the hole disappeared beneath the water, which rushed into her and turned her completely over. A minute and a half, and all that could be seen of the *Queen Mary* was her keel, and then that disappeared.

In the course of the day our destroyers picked up two survivors of the *Queen Mary*, a mid-shipman and a seaman, and brought them as prisoners of war to Wilhelmshaven. According to their account there were more than 1,400 men on the *Queen Mary*, among whom was a Japanese prince, the Naval *Attaché* in London. The captain of the *Queen Mary* was Captain C. J. Prowse.

In their list of officer losses the Admiralty said, speaking of the *Queen Mary*:

> With the exception of four midshipmen all officers on board were lost.

Scarcely had the *Queen Mary* disappeared in the cloud of smoke when I began to find a new target with my periscope. I veered the periscope to the left and saw to my astonishment that there were still two battle-cruisers there.

It was not until this moment that I realized that hitherto I had been engaging the third ship in the line. The *Lion*, then, had meanwhile taken station again at the head of the enemy line. Our target was once more the *Princess Royal*.

After the destruction of the *Queen Mary* the following orders were recorded in the fore-control:

Time, h. m. s.	Training angle.	Range in m.	Deflection.	Orders for elevation telegraphs, etc.
6 27 15	47°	12,200	left 12	Fire ! 2 short !
6 28 –	60°	12,400	,, 14	4 short !
6 28 30	83°	12,600		
6 29 20	88°	14,000	,, 14	
6 30 20	88°	14,600	,, 10	4 short !
6 31 20	87°	15,000		
6 32 10	87°	15,700	,, 2	4 short !
6 33 10	105°	16,400		

One minute five seconds, therefore, after the last salvo struck the *Queen Mary*, the first salvo struck the *Princess Royal*. I had had the range of this ship measured by the Bg. man in the fore-control. The measured range was only 12,200 m. At this range I fired the first salvo, which fell short. The same thing happened with the next two salvoes, so that I increased the range considerably for the fourth. The Bg. man had apparently not realized that after the sinking of the *Queen Mary* the range no longer decreased but began to increase rapidly. The continually changing training angle recorded in the log shows that the ship was steering a very irregular course and was bearing to port. The enemy's bearing was now somewhat more abaft the beam. This put successful rapid shooting out of the question. As a rule there was a full minute between the salvoes. Each time we had to wait for the splashes. When these were ob-served new orders had generally to be given for deflection, rate and elevation.

At 6.36 p.m. the range was 16,800 m.

Meanwhile we saw that the enemy were being reinforced. Behind the battle-cruiser line appeared four big ships. We soon identified these as of the *Queen Elizabeth* class. There had been much talk in our fleet of these ships. They were ships of the line with the colossal armament of eight 15-in. guns, 28,000 tons displacement and a speed of twenty-five knots. Their speed, therefore, was scarcely inferior to ours (twenty-six knots), but they fired a shell more than twice as heavy as ours. They engaged at portentous ranges. We were now being subjected to heavy fire and so we steered a zigzag course.

Between 6.36 and 6.45 p.m. I did not fire the heavy guns at all. The reason for this lay for the most part with the smoke from the destroyer action which was still raging between the lines, and our anti-destroyer fire which was being controlled by the Third Gunnery Officer, Lieutenant-Commander Hausser. The English destroyers had by now pressed forward infernally near to us.

As I could see nothing of the big ships I had ample opportunity of observing the course of this action. It was a wonderful spectacle, when the *Regensburg*, flying the flag of Commodore Heinrich, formerly my commanding officer on the *Derfflinger*, passed through our line at the head of a flotilla all firing furiously. Our destroyers and those of the enemy closed one another to the shortest range. I saw two of our destroyers fall out. They were leaking badly and it was obvious that it was all up with them. Others went alongside under fire and took off the entire ship's company. One English destroyer sank and others hauled out, out of control. Meanwhile our 15-cm. salvoes crashed out unceasingly, Lieutenant-Commander Hausser very effectively straddling several destroyers, which he engaged one after the other. On one he registered a visible hit; she stopped suddenly and then disappeared in a cloud of smoke.

What a pity it was that there was no marine artist on board! The well-known marine painter Klaus Bergen had often accompanied us on our sweeps in the North Sea. This time something had prevented his coming. He regretted this very much afterwards, but in spite of his absence he became the most successful painter of the Skagerrak battle. Unfortunately photography on board was strictly forbidden. Cameras were not allowed in the ships. This was a precaution against espionage. As a result, not a single photograph was taken of the Battle of Skagerrak in the whole German fleet.

The log-keeper in the secondary armament transmitting station, Midshipman Hauth, who kept an admirable log throughout the whole action, recorded as follows for the time of the destroyer repulse:

6.37 p.m.: Secondary armament on destroyers! As directed! 6,000! On the destroyer to extreme left! Fire!—7,000!—Fire!—6,400! Fire!—6,000—Fire—Fire—Good, Rapid!—Fire—Fire—Fire!
6.42 p.m.: Secondary armament, cease fire—-6,800—Fire—5,500—Fire—5,000—Fire—Fire—5,600—Fire—Fire!—7,000—Fire—6,800—Fire!—Good, Rapid!—Fire—Fire—Fire!—7,000—Fire—Fire!
6.45 p.m.: Ship turning to port!—Fire!—8,000—Fire!—8,400—Fire—Fire!
6.48 p.m.: Secondary armament, cease fire!"

At 6.48 p.m. the anti-destroyer fire broke off and at 6.50 p.m. the whole squadron altered course to N.N.W. With this manoeuvre Admiral Hipper with the battle-cruisers took a position about seven sea miles in advance of the head of our main fleet, who were steering approximately a N.N.W. course at full speed and whose head soon afterwards engaged the ships of the *Queen Elizabeth* class.

From numerous hits with 10.5-cm. shell we ascertained later that the English destroyers had also subjected us to a heavy fire. In the general uproar of the battle this had escaped my notice. The 10.5-cm. shell were, of course, entirely ineffective against our armour; they had only taken effect in the unprotected parts of the ship, particularly in the rigging, where they had damaged our wireless aerials and some of the gunnery telephone wires in the tops. After the action an officer found an unexploded 10.5-cm. shell in his bunk when he was turning in.

Between 6.45 and 6.50 p.m. I fired eight more salvoes with the heavy guns at 18,000 m. at the Princess Royal, but without any particular success .

As we were altering course to N.N.W. we caught sight of the head of our 3rd Squadron, the proud ships of the *König* class. Everyone now breathed more freely. While we had been engaged by the English 5th Battle Squadron with its 15-in. guns in addition to the Battle Cruiser Squadron we had felt rather uncomfortable.

At 6.50 p.m. I sent the following message to the guns:

Ship slowly bearing to starboard. Our 3rd Squadron has come up.

This closed the first phase of the battle. We had seen one English giant blown to pieces by our fire like a barrel of gunpowder. The *Derfflinger*, however, had come out of the engagement with her fighting strength unimpaired. What wonder that we were in high spirits and looked forward confidently to the next action! We were now in close touch with our most powerful battle squadron and we thought that we were only opposed to the four remaining battle-cruisers and the four ships of the *Queen Elizabeth* class. We were filled with the proud joy of victory and hoped to accomplish the destruction of the whole force opposed to us. We had acquired an absolute confidence in our ship. It seemed quite out of the question that our proud ship could be shattered in a few minutes like the *Queen Mary* and the *Indefatigable*.

On the other hand, I had a feeling that we could blow up any English ship in no time, given a straight course for a time and not too long a range—if possible not over 15,000 m. We were burning to win fresh laurels. One could feel that a feeling of exaltation reigned throughout the ship. The gun crews had done their work with incredible efficiency and even during the most rapid fire had always had their guns ready as soon as the fire-gong rang. The gun-barrels began to get very hot after an hour's firing, the grey paint began to blister and to turn brown and yellow. The coolness with which the captain commanded the ship had been exemplary. He had frequently helped me with messages, but for the rest had left me a free hand, particularly as to choice of targets.

CHAPTER 7

The Second Phase of the Skagerrak Battle (6.55 to 7.5 p.m.)

The second phase was just as unsatisfactory as the first was successful and interesting from the point of view of gunnery. The enemy had learned a devil of a lesson and acquired a deep respect for the effectiveness of our gunfire. During the wild dash north they kept as much as possible out of our range, but kept us within reach of their own long-range guns. It will be seen from Sketch 1 (p. 105). that in this second phase the ranges are scarcely ever less than 18,000 m. I only fired to make quite sure that the enemy were still out of range, and then, to save ammunition, I contented myself with isolated shots from one turret. The guns were again trained on the upper edge of the funnels or the mastheads.

At these long ranges the enemy's shooting was not good either, though their salvoes, it is true, fell well together and always over an area of not more than three hundred to four hundred metres diameter. The control, however, was not very efficient, perhaps owing to the poor visibility. At any rate, the salvoes fell at very irregular distances from our ship. Nevertheless, we suffered bad hits, two or three heavy shells striking us during this phase. When a heavy shell hit the armour of our ship, the terrific crash of the explosion was followed by a vibration of the whole ship, affecting even the conning-tower. The shells which exploded in the interior of the ship caused rather a dull roar, which was trans-mitted all over by the countless voice-pipes and telephones.

The four English battle-cruisers were travelling at top speed, and it was not long before they vanished from our view in mist and smoke. They were steering north and our inferior speed made it impossible for us to keep up with them, though at 7.21 p.m. the commander-in-chief of the fleet signalled: "Follow the battle-cruisers." Our Battle Cruiser Squadron, however, could not maintain a speed of more than twenty-five knots for any length of time, and with their speed of twenty-eight knots the English ships left us standing.

At the time we did not grasp the object of the enemy's manoeuvre. We assumed that they were merely trying to get into touch quickly with their main fleet, whose presence we inferred from the movements of the English battle-cruisers. Actually Admiral Beatty, by completely outflanking us in spite of our highest speed, accomplished an excellent tactical manoeuvre, and his ships carried out an admirable feat of technique.

He accomplished the famous "crossing the T," compelled us to alter course, and finally brought us into such a position that we were completely enveloped by the English Battle Fleet and the English battle-cruisers. In the later phases of the battle we were, as a rule, no longer able to tell to which enemy ship we were opposed, and I cannot therefore say with any certainty when we engaged Beatty's four battle-cruisers again, or if we ever did so.

After the gradual disappearance of the four battle-cruisers we were still faced with the four powerful ships of the Fifth Battle Squadron, *Malaya*, *Valiant*, *Barham* and *Warspite*.

These ships cannot have developed very high speed in this phase of the battle, for they soon came within range of our 3rd Squadron, and were engaged by the ships at the head of the line, particularly the flagship, the *König*. In this way the four English battleships at one time and another came under the fire of at least nine German ships, five battle-cruisers and from four to five battleships. According to my gunnery-log, we were firing after 7.16 p.m. at the second battleship from the right, the one immediately astern of the leader. At these great ranges I fired armour-piercing shell.

The second phase passed without any important events as far as we were concerned. In a sense, this part of the action, fought against a numerically inferior but more powerfully armed enemy, who kept us under fire at ranges at which we were helpless, was highly depressing, nerve-wracking and exasperating. Our only means of defence was to leave the line for a short time, when we saw that the enemy had our range. As this manoeuvre was imperceptible to the enemy, we extricated ourselves at regular intervals from the hail of fire.

I may remark here that these slight alterations of course to get out of the enemy's fire are not shown on the sketch, as we always took station again in the line at top speed immediately afterwards.

It was not long before the gunnery conditions underwent a fundamental change.

ENGLISH BATTLE-CRUISER *QUEEN MARY*, SUNK AT 6.26 P. M. ON THE 31ST MAY, 1916

CHAPTER 8

Third Phase of the Skagerrak Battle
(7.50 to 9.5 p.m.)

At 7.40 p.m. enemy light cruisers and destroyers launched a tor-pedo attack against us. We therefore altered course to N.N.E., *i.e.*, about six points to starboard.

The visibility was now so bad that it was difficult for us to distin-guish the enemy ships. We were engaging light cruisers and destroyers. At 7.55 p.m. we turned on an easterly course, and at 8 p.m. the whole Battle Cruiser Squadron formed a line of bearing on a southerly course as the destroyers pressed home the attack. This brought us very effectively out of the line of the torpedoes that had been fired against us. At 8.12 p.m. we again altered course towards the enemy. During this time we had only fired intermittently with our heavy and second-ary armament. At 8.15 p.m. we came under heavy fire. It flashed out on all sides. We could only make out the ships' hulls indistinctly, but as far as I was able to see the horizon, enemy ships were all round us. As I could not distinguish either the end or the beginning of the enemy line, I was unable to engage the "second ship from the right," but se-lected the one I could see best.

And now a terrific struggle began. Within a short time the din of the battle reached a climax. It was now perfectly clear to us that we were faced with the whole English Fleet. I could see from her gigan-tic hull that I had engaged a giant battleship. Between the two lines light cruiser and destroyer actions were still raging. All at once I saw through my periscope a German light cruiser passing us in flames. I recognized the *Wiesbaden*. She was almost hidden in smoke, with only the quarter-deck clear, and her after-gun firing incessantly at an Eng-lish cruiser. Gallant *Wiesbaden*! Gallant crew!

The only survivor was Chief Stoker Zenne, who was picked up by a Norwegian fishing boat after drifting about for three days on a raft; all the rest, including the poet, Gorch Fock, who loved the sea above all else, sealed their loyalty to their *Kaiser* and Empire by a sailor's death. The *Wiesbaden* was subjected to a heavy fire by an English light cruiser. Again and again her shells struck the poor *Wiesbaden*. Seized with fury, I abandoned my former target, had the English cruiser's range measured, gave the range and deflection, and "*crash!*"—a salvo roared out at the *Wiesbaden's* tormentor. One more salvo and I had him. A column of smoke rose high in the air. Apparently a magazine had exploded. The cruiser turned away and hauled out at top speed, while I peppered her with two or three more salvoes.

At this moment Lieut.-Commander Hausser, who had been engaging destroyers with his secondary armament, asked me: "Is this cruiser with four funnels German or English, sir?" I examined the ship through the periscope. In the misty grey light the colours of the German and English ships were difficult to distinguish. The cruiser was not very far away from us. She had four funnels and two masts, like our *Rostock*.

"She is certainly English," Lieutenant-Commander Hausser shouted. "May I fire?"

"Yes, fire away." I was now certain she was a big English ship. The secondary armament was trained on the new target. Lieutenant-Commander Hausser gave the order: "6,000!" Then, just as he was about to give the order: "Fire!" something terrific happened: the English ship, which I had meanwhile identified as an old English armoured cruiser, broke in half with a tremendous explosion. Black smoke and *débris* shot into the air, a flame enveloped the whole ship, and then she sank before our eyes. There was nothing but a gigantic smoke cloud to mark the place where just before a proud ship had been fighting. I think she was destroyed by the fire of our next ahead, Admiral Hipper's flagship, the *Lützow*.

This all happened in a much shorter time than I have taken to tell it. The whole thing was over in a few seconds, and then we had already engaged new targets. The destroyed ship was the *Defence*, an old armoured cruiser of the same class as the *Black Prince*, which was sunk on the following night by the *Thüringen* and other ships of the line. She was a ship of 14,800 tons, armed with six 23.4-cm. and ten 15.2-cm. guns, and carrying a crew of 700 men. Not one of the whole ship's company was saved. She was blown to atoms and all the men were killed by the explosion. As we saw the ship at a comparatively short distance in good visibility, magnified fifteen times by the periscopes, we could see exactly what happened. The whole horror of this event is indelibly fixed on my mind.

I went on to engage other big ships, without any idea what kind of ships they were. At 8.22 p.m. we turned on a south-easterly course, but in the general confusion of the battle that was now raging I had lost all grasp of the tactical situation. Once the thought flashed across my mind: "Can we be firing at German ships?" At that moment, however, the visibility, which changed from one minute to the next, but which on the whole was gradually growing worse, improved and revealed distinctly the typical English silhouette and dark grey colour. It is my opinion that our light grey colour was more favourable than the dark grey of the English ships. Our ships were much more quickly concealed by the thin films of mist which were now driving across the sea from east to west.

At 8.25 p.m. Lieutenant von der Decken, in the after-control, recorded: "*Lützow* heavily hit forward. Ship on fire. Much smoke. "At 8.30 p.m. he wrote: "Three heavy hits on the *Derfflinger*" Of these one hit the 15-cm. battery on the port side, went clean through the centre gun and burst, killing or wounding the whole of the casemate crew. The explosion also knocked the first 15-cm. gun off its mounting and killed or wounded several men. The other hits were aft.

I now selected my target as far ahead as possible, the leading ship of the enemy line, for I saw that the *Lützow's* fire was now weak. At times the smoke from her burning forepart made fire-control on the *Lützow* impossible.

At 8.24 p.m. I began to engage large enemy battleships to the north-east. Even though the ranges were short, from 6,000 to 7,000 m., the ships often became invisible in the slowly advancing mists, mixed with the smoke from the guns and funnels. It was almost impossible to observe the splashes. All splashes that fell over could not be seen at all, and only those that fell very short could be distinguished clearly, which was not much help, for as soon as we got nearer the target again it became impossible to see where the shots fell. I was shooting by the measurements of the Bg. man in the fore-control, Leading Seaman Hänel, who had been my loyal servant for five years. In view of the misty weather these measurements were very irregular and inexact, but as no observation was possible I had no alternative.

Meanwhile we were being subjected to a heavy, accurate and rapid fire from several ships at the same time. It was clear that the enemy could now see us much better than we could see them. This will be difficult to understand for anyone who does not know the sea, but it is a fact that in this sort of weather the differences in visibility are very great in different directions. A ship clear of the mist is much more clearly visible from a ship actually in the mist than *vice versa*. In determining visibility an important part is played by the position of the sun. In misty weather the ships with their shady side towards the enemy are much easier to see than those lit by the sun.

In this way a severe, unequal struggle developed. Several heavy shells pierced our ship with terrific force and exploded with a tremendous roar, which shook every seam and rivet. The captain had again frequently to steer the ship out of the line in order to get out of the hail of fire. It was pretty heavy shooting.

This went on until 8.29 p.m.

At this moment the veil of mist in front of us split across like the curtain at a theatre. Clear and sharply silhouetted against the uncovered part of the horizon we saw a powerful battleship with two funnels between the masts and a third close against the forward tripod mast. She was steering an almost parallel course with ours at top speed. Her guns were trained on us and immediately another salvo crashed out, straddling us completely. "Range 9,000!" roared Leading Seaman Hänel.

"9,000—Salvoes-fire!" I ordered, and with feverish anxiety I waited for our splashes.

"Over. Two hits!" called out Lieutenant-Commander von Stosch.

I gave the order: "100 down. Good, Rapid!" and thirty seconds after the first salvo the second left the guns. I observed two short splashes and two hits.

Lieutenant-Commander von Stosch called: "Hits!" Every twenty seconds came the roar of another salvo. At 8.31 p.m. the *Derfflinger* fired her last salvo at this ship, and then for the third time we witnessed the dreadful spectacle that we had already seen in the case of the *Queen Mary* and the *Defence*.

As with the other ships there occurred a rapid succession of heavy explosions, masts collapsed, debris was hurled into the air, a gigantic column of black smoke rose towards the sky, and from the parting sections of the ship, coal dust spurted in all directions. Flames enveloped the ship, fresh explosions followed, and behind this murky shroud our enemy vanished from our sight. I shouted into the telephone: "Our enemy has blown up!" and above the din of the battle a great cheer thundered through the ship and was transmitted to the fore-control by all the gunnery telephones and flashed from one gun-position to another. I sent up a short, fervent prayer of thanks to the Almighty, shouted to my servant: "Bravo, Hänel, jolly well measured!" and then my order rang out: "Change target to the left. On the second battle-cruiser from the right!" The battle continued.

Who was this enemy? I had not examined her carefully nor given much thought to her identity, but I had taken her to be an English battle-cruiser. I described her as such in giving the target, as my gunnery log-keeper recorded. There had been no time to discuss her class while we were engaging her, for there had only been a few minutes in which to recognize her with any certainty. Only the gunnery officers and gun-layers and the torpedo-officers had seen her blow up, the attention of the captain and his assistants, the navigating and signal officers being entirely taken up with keeping the ship in her station. It was difficult work navigating astern of the *Lützow*, which was hardly in a condition to keep her place in the line.

When, after the battle, the reports came to be drawn up, most of the officers were convinced that she was a ship of the *Queen Elizabeth* class. I was of the opinion that she belonged to the *Invincible* class, but I admitted that I was not at all sure. If you take a naval pocket-book and compare the silhouettes of the *Queen Elizabeth* and *Invincible* classes, there is at first sight a perplexing similarity. We therefore entered in our report that at 8.30 p.m. we had destroyed by gunfire a battleship of the *Queen Elizabeth* class. Our report ran:

The ship blew up in a similar way to the *Queen Mary* at 6.26 p.m. Clearly observed by the First and Third Gunnery Officers, and the First Torpedo Officer in the fore-control, the Second and Fourth Gunnery Officers in the after control and the Gunnery Observation Officer in the fore-top. Ship of the *Queen Elizabeth* class.

After the battle, the following statement was made by English prisoners at Wilhelmshaven:

One of the *Queen Elizabeth* ships, the *Warspite*, left the line, listing heavily, and hauled away to the north-west. At 8 p.m. the English destroyer *Turbulent* received a wireless report that the *Warspite* had sunk.

On the strength of our battle report and the statements of the prisoners, our Admiralty authorities were obliged to assume that the ship destroyed by the *Derfflinger* was the *Warspite*, and, accordingly, the *Warspite* instead of the *Invincible* was reported as an enemy loss. That the *Invincible* was sunk we learned from the report of the English Admiralty, and naturally her loss was added afterwards to the previous report. As a matter of fact, it was the *Invincible* we had engaged and blown up and not the *Warspite*. The English reports soon made this quite clear.

On the 3rd June, the *Manchester Guardian* said that the German Admiralty report of the 1st June contained a detailed and frankly exact report of the English losses, except that it gave the name of the battle-ship *Warspite* instead of the battle-cruiser *Invincible*.

The Times of 6th June, 1916, reports on the evidence of combatants: "The *Invincible*, flying the flag of Admiral Hood, Sir David Beatty's second in command, singled out the *Hindenburg*, and after a hot fight, in which some of our men claim that the Hindenburg received mortal injury, the *Invincible* went down."

At this time the *Hindenburg* was still being built. The *Derfflinger* was her sister-ship and the English account is correct but for the names: it was the *Derfflinger* and not the still uncompleted *Hindenburg* that engaged the Invincible.

The account of the engagement between the *Derfflinger* and the *Invincible* given by one of the two officers saved from the *Invincible* is perfectly correct with the exception of the time. *The Times* of the 12th June, 1916, reports that the father of a lieutenant who went down with the *Invincible* received from the two surviving officers a letter, in which they say:

> Your son was with the Admiral and we were engaged with the *Derfflinger*. There was a tremendous explosion aboard at 6.34 p.m. The ship broke in half and sank in ten or fifteen seconds.

On the 13th June, 1916, *The Times*, quoting a letter from the brother of the late Lieutenant Charles Fisher says:

> We learn from Commander Dannreuther, the sole surviving officer of H.M.S. *Invincible*, that a shell fell into the powder-magazine. There was a great explosion, and when Dannreuther recovered consciousness he found himself in the water. Ship and crew had disappeared.

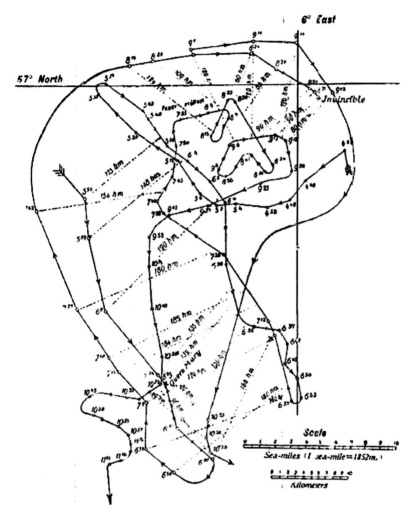

Course of the *Derfflinger* and other German Battle-Cruisers during the Battle of Skagerrak.

— Approximate Course of English Battleships engaged by the *Derfflinger*.

..... Direction and Range of the *Derfflinger's* Heavy Guns.

That they were the ships of Hood's battle-cruiser squadron that we had been engaging from 8. 24 p.m. onwards, at ranges varying between 6,000 m. and 7,000 m., is confirmed by Admiral Beatty's official dispatch. This reports as follows on the part played by the *Invincible*, *Indomitable* and *Inflexible* of the 3rd Battle Cruiser Squadron:

> At 6.20 p.m. the 3rd Battle Cruiser Squadron appeared ahead, steaming south towards the enemy's van. I ordered them to take station ahead, which was carried out magnificently, Rear-Admiral Hood bringing his squadron into action in a most inspiring manner, worthy of his great naval ancestors. At 6.25 p.m. I altered course to the E.S.E. in support of the 3rd Battle Cruiser Squadron, who were at this time only 8,000 yards from the enemy's leading ship. They were pouring a hot fire into her and caused her to turn to the westward of south.

A Reuter telegram of the 5th June, 1916, states that when the action had been in progress some hours the *Indomitable*, *Invincible* and *Inflexible* appeared on the scene; that this phase was chiefly a duel of heavy guns and that the *Invincible*, after fighting bravely and inflicting heavy punishment on the enemy, met her doom and sank.

My reason for supporting my own description of this event from the English accounts of the battle is that, hitherto, the German reports have left it open as to whether the sinking of the *Invincible* was due to gunfire or a torpedo. On historical grounds I consider it necessary to make clear that the *Invincible*, like all the other English ships lost in this battle, was destroyed by gunfire.

The officer commanding the 3rd Battle Cruiser Squadron, Rear-Admiral Hood, who went down in the *Invincible*, was a descendant of the famous English Admiral Hood, who distinguished himself brilliantly as a strategist and tactician in the North American War of Independence under Graves and Rodney, and later as commander-in-chief at the Battle of St. Christopher (1782). During the Anglo-French War of 1793-1802 he was Commander-in-Chief (1793-1794) of the Mediterranean Fleet and bombarded Toulon.

According to the record of my log-keeper the heavy guns fired until 8.33 p.m. At 8.38 p.m. I gave the order: "Heavy guns stand by!" There was no longer any enemy to be seen. At 8.35 p.m. we had altered course sharply to the west. After the loss of their leader the remaining ships of the 3rd Battle Squadron did not immediately venture into the zone of our death-dealing fire. At 8.50 p.m. the whole ship was ordered to cease fire. Then feverish efforts were made to put out the fires that had broken out in various parts of the ship.

At this time we noticed a destroyer slowly going alongside the *Lützow*. The flagship had a list, that is to say, she was leaning over to one side, and her bows were very deep in the water. Great clouds of smoke were rising from her forepart. Admiral Hipper boarded the destroyer, which then cast off and steered for the *Seydlitz*. While passing the *Derfflinger* the Admiral signalled: "Captain of the *Derfflinger* will take command until I board." Our captain was therefore in command of the battle-cruisers until nearly 11 p.m., for, owing to the headlong speed of the battle-cruisers, which were almost continuously under enemy fire, it was not until then that the Admiral succeeded in boarding another ship.

The *Derfflinger*, too, was now a pretty sorry sight. The masts and rigging had been badly damaged by countless shells, and the wireless aerials hung down in an inextricable tangle so that we could only use our wireless for receiving; we could not transmit messages. A heavy shell had torn away two armour plates in the bows, leaving a huge gap quite 6 by 5 m., just above the water-line. With the pitching of the ship water streamed continually through this hole.

While we were steering west the commander came on to the bridge and reported to the captain: "The ship must stop at once. The after torpedo-net has been shot away and is hanging over the port screw. It must be cleared." The captain gave the order: "All engines stop!"

I surveyed the horizon through the periscope. There was nothing of the enemy to be seen at this moment. The *Seydlitz*, *Moltke* and *Von der Tann* were not in very close touch with us, but they now came up quickly and took their prescribed stations in the line. It was a very serious matter that we should have to stop like this in the immediate neighbourhood of the enemy, but if the torpedo-net were to foul the screw all would be up with us. How many times we had cursed in the ship at not having rid ourselves of these heavy steel torpedo-nets, weighing several hundred tons. As we hardly ever anchored at sea they were useless and, in any case, they only protected part of the ship against torpedo fire. On the other hand, they were a serious source of danger, as they reduced the ship's speed considerably and were bound sooner or later to foul the screws, which meant the loss of the ship. For these reasons the English had scrapped their torpedo-nets shortly before the war—we did not do so until immediately after the Battle of Skagerrak and as a result of our present experience.

The boatswain and the turret-crews of the "Dora" and "Caesar" turrets, under Lieutenant-Commander Boltenstern, worked like furies to lift the net, make it fast with chains and cut with axes the wire-hawsers and chains that were hanging loose. It was only a few minutes before the report came: "Engines can be started." We got under weigh at once.

The *Lützow* had now hauled out of the line and was steering a southerly course at low speed. The captain wanted to signal to the other ships to follow the leader, but all the signal apparatus was out of action. The semaphores and heliographs had all been shot away and the flags all destroyed by fire. However, our stout ships followed without signal when the captain turned on a northerly course and led the battle-cruisers to a position ahead of the main fleet.

The lull in the battle lasted until 9.5 p.m. and then suddenly fresh gunfire flashed out and once more the cry, "Clear for action!" rang through the ship.

English Battle-Cruiser *Invincible*, sunk at 8.31 p. m. on the 31st May, 1916

CHAPTER 9

The Fourth Phase of the Skagerrak Battle (9.5 p.m. to 9.37 p.m.)

The previous phases of the battle had been a glorious progress from one triumph to another. We had experienced all the wild splendour of a sea action. Now we were not to be spared its terrors. During the lull in the fighting I had remained on the bridge without removing my head-telephone. "Where are the enemy?" I shouted, when I was back at my periscope.

"Light cruisers on the port beam!" was reported. In order to spare the heavy guns for more important targets, I ordered Lieutenant-Commander Hausser to engage the light cruisers with the 15-cm. guns. He opened fire at 7,000. Meanwhile I scanned the horizon. As there were no other ships in sight, I also opened fire with the heavy guns at one of the ships reported as light cruisers. The enemy ships were again at the extreme limit of visibility. Now they opened a lively fire, and I saw that the ship I had selected as a target was firing full salvoes from four double turrets. The light round the enemy cleared for a moment and I saw distinctly that they were battleships of the heaviest class, with 38-cm. guns! Fire was now flashing from them.

Meanwhile the commander-in-chief had realized the danger to which our fleet was exposed. The van of our fleet was shut in by the semicircle of the enemy. We were in a regular death-trap. There was only one way of escape from this unfavourable tactical situation: to turn the line about and withdraw on the opposite course. Before everything we must get out of this dangerous enemy envelopment. But this manoeuvre had to be carried out unnoticed and unhindered. The battle-cruisers and the destroyers had to cover the movements of the fleet. At about 9.12 p.m. the commander-in-chief gave the fleet the signal to turn about on the opposite course and almost at the same time sent by wireless to the battle-cruisers and destroyers the historic order: "Close the enemy." The signal man on our bridge read the message aloud, adding the words, which stood against it in the signal book: "And ram! The ships will fight to the death."

Without moving an eyelid the captain gave the order: "Full speed ahead. Course S.E." Followed by the *Seydlitz, Moltke* and *Von der Tann*, we altered course south at 9.15 p.m. and headed straight for the enemy's van. The *Derfflinger*, as leading ship, now came under a particularly deadly fire. Several ships were engaging us at the same time. I selected a target and fired as rapidly as possible. At first the ranges recorded by my faithful log-keeper in the transmitting station were 12,000, from which they sank to 8,000. And all the time we were steaming at full speed into this inferno, offering a splendid target to the enemy while they were still hard to make out. Commander Scheibe, in his description of the battle, describes this attack as follows:

> The battle-cruisers, temporarily under the command of the Captain of the *Derfflinger*, while Admiral Hipper was changing ship, now hurled themselves recklessly against the enemy line, followed by the destroyers. A dense hail of fire swept them all the way.

Salvo after salvo fell round us, hit after hit struck our ship. They were stirring minutes. My communication with Lieutenant-Commander von Stosch was now cut off, the telephones and speaking-tubes running to the fore-top having been shot away. I was now left to rely entirely on my own observation of the splashes to control the gun-fire. Hitherto I had continued to fire with all four heavy turrets, but at 9.13 p.m. a serious catastrophe occurred. A 38-cm. shell pierced the armour of the "Caesar" turret and exploded inside. The brave turret commander, Lieutenant-Commander von Boltenstern had both his legs torn off and with him nearly the whole gun crew was killed. The shell set on fire two shell-cases in the turret. The flames from the burning cases spread to the transfer chamber, where it set fire to four more cases, and from there to the case-chamber, where four more were ignited.

The burning cartridge-cases emitted great tongues of flame which shot up out of the turrets as high as a house; but they only blazed, they did not explode as had been the case with the enemy. This saved the ship, but the result of the fire was catastrophic. The huge tapering flames killed everyone within their reach. Of the seventy-eight men inside the turret only five managed to save themselves through the hole provided for throwing out empty shell-cases, and of these several were severely injured. The other seventy-three men died together like heroes in the fierce fever of battle, loyally obeying the orders of their turret officer.

A few moments later this catastrophe was followed by a second. A 38-cm. shell pierced the roof of the "Dora" turret, and here too, exploded inside the turret. The same horrors ensued. With the exception of one single man, who was thrown by the concussion through the turret entrance, the whole turret crew of eighty men, including all the magazine men, were killed instantly. The crew of the "Dora" turret, under the leadership of their brave turret officer, *Stückmeister* Arndt, had fought heroically up to the last second. Here, too, the flames spread to the cartridge-chamber and set fire to all the cases which had been removed from their protective packing. From both after-turrets great flames were now spurting, mingled with clouds of yellow smoke, two ghastly pyres.

At 9.15 p.m. I received a message from the transmitting station: "Gas danger in the heavy gun transmitting station. Station must be abandoned." This gave me a shock. Things must be in a pretty bad way in the ship if the poison gases had already penetrated the transmitting station, which was so carefully protected. I gave the order: "Connect with the fore-control," and at once received the report that the gunnery apparatus was actually connected with the fore-control before the transmitting station was abandoned. I could now control the guns by shouting my orders through a speaking tube to a messenger who sat under a grating. The latter passed on the orders direct to the gun-turrets by means of his gunnery telephones and telegraphs. This, of course, added to the noise of the shouting in the fore-control, but made it possible to go on with the fire control.

Now hit after hit shook the ship. The enemy had got our range excellently. I felt a clutch at my heart when I thought of what the conditions must be in the interior of the ship. So far we in the armoured tower had come off very well . . . my train of thought was sharply interrupted. Suddenly, we seemed to hear the crack of doom. A terrific roar, a tremendous explosion and then darkness, in which we felt a colossal blow. The whole conning tower seemed to be hurled into the air as though by the hands of some portentous giant, and then to flutter trembling into its former position. A heavy shell had struck the fore-control about 50 cm. in front of me. The shell exploded, but failed to pierce the thick armour, which it had struck at an unfavourable angle, though huge pieces had been torn out. Poisonous greenish-yellow gases poured through the apertures into our control.

I called out: "Down gas-masks!" and immediately every man pulled down his gas-mask over his face. I went on controlling the fire with my gas-mask on, which made it very difficult to make myself understood. But the gases soon dissipated, and we cautiously took off the masks. We assured ourselves that the gunnery apparatus was still in order. Nothing had been disturbed. Even the delicate mechanism of the sighting apparatus was, strange to say, still in order. Some splinters had been flung through the aperture on to the bridge, where they had wounded several men, including the navigating officer.

The terrific blow had burst open the heavy armoured door of the tower, which now stood wide open. Two men strove in vain to force it back, but it was jammed too tight. Then came unexpected assistance. Once more we heard a colossal roar and crash and with a noise of a bursting thunderbolt a 38-cm. shell exploded under the bridge. Whole sheets of the deck were hurled through the air, a tremendous concussion threw overboard everything that could be moved. Amongst other things, the chart house, with all the charts and other gear, and—*last but not least*—my good overcoat, which I had left hanging in the chart house, vanished from the scene for ever. And one extraordinary thing happened: the terrific concussion of the bursting 38-cm. shell shut the armoured door of the fore-control. A polite race, the English! They had opened the door for us and it was they who shut it again. I wonder if they meant to? In any case it amused us a good deal.

I looked towards the enemy through my periscope. Their salvoes were still bursting round us, but we could scarcely see anything of the enemy, who were disposed in a great semicircle round us. All we could see was the great reddish-gold flames spurting from the guns. The ships' hulls we saw but rarely. I had the range of the flames measured. That was the only possible means of establishing the enemy's range. With-out much hope of hurting the enemy I ordered the two forward turrets to fire salvo after salvo. I could feel that our fire soothed the nerves of the ship's company. If we had ceased fire at this time the whole ship's company would have been overwhelmed by despair, for everyone would have thought: "A few minutes more and it will be all up." But so long as we were still firing, things could not be so bad. The secondary armament were firing too, but of the six guns on that side only two could be used. The barrel of the fourth gun had burst, and the third gun had been completely shot to pieces. The two 15-cm. guns still intact kept up a lively fire.

Unfortunately the direction-indicator in the "Bertha" turret now failed us. I was left with one single turret that I could train on the enemy by means of my periscope. The direction of my periscope as indicated by the control apparatus had to be continually shouted from the transmitting station to the "Bertha" turret, which meant a certain amount of delay for the turret officer, and was, of course, inadequate, while the ship was under weigh. The turret officer was not in a position to keep the enemy under continual observation with his telescope. Nothing could be seen of the monster facing us but the flickering fiery eyes it opened alternately—when it fired a salvo. I was now concentrating my fire on a ship which was firing alternately from two double turrets.

The flashes from the muzzles looked like the opening of two wide blazing eyes and suddenly I realized where I had seen something of the sort. Sascha Schneider's picture, "The feeling of dependence," had created an impression something similar to that I was now experiencing. It depicts a black monster of shadowy outline, turgidly opening and shutting its smouldering eyes and fixing a chained human form, which awaits the fatal embrace. Our present position seemed to me similar. But the monster had to be fought. The "Anna" turret, under the brave *Stückmeister*—I had sent the turret officer to the after control to replace the Fourth Gunnery Officer who was wanted elsewhere—went on firing undisturbed, as also the doughty "Schülzburg," though it is true, the latter frequently fired at another target than that ordered. Without a direction-indicator it was impossible to keep both turrets firing at the same enemy flashes.

At 9.18 p.m. we received a wireless message from the commander-in-chief: "Manoeuvre on the enemy van." That meant we were to break off our charge against the enemy and carry on a running engagement with the ships of the enemy's van. We therefore turned to the south of westward. Unfortunately the enemy were now so far abaft the beam that in my forward position I could no longer see them. Now the control had to be shifted aft. But the necessary readjustment of connections could only be carried out in the transmitting station. At the time this was not possible. There was no possibility for the moment of directing the two forward turrets, which were now the only ones available.

I gave the order: "Turrets independent," and for a time the two turrets fired independently, under the control of their turret officers. I observed that the "Bertha" turret soon got the range of the target far astern and maintained a lively fire in which the "Anna" turret was soon participating. For some time the enemy was dead astern of us, so that the forward turrets lost sight of him, for their angle of training was limited to 220°. We were now helpless! As we turned, the torpedo officer fired a torpedo at 8,000 m. At the same time our destroyers, which until then had been following in our wake, pressed home their attack, several flotillas together. A dense smoke rose between us and the enemy "monsters."

Once more we watched the wild turmoil of battle before us. It was hard to distinguish friend from foe. More and more destroyers dashed into the fray, disappeared in the smoke and then for a few moments were visible again. Others which had already fired their torpedoes were beginning to return. After the attack the flotillas reassembled behind us and then attacked a second time. The enemy now disappeared from our view and their fire ceased as far as we were concerned. We breathed a sigh of relief! The enemy fire thundered and roared on all sides, it is true, but we were no longer the target. As my gunnery log-keeper had to evacuate the transmitting station at 9.15 p.m. no log for this phase of the battle was kept subsequent to this time.

At 9.23 p.m. a report came from the transmitting station: "Transmitting station untenable!" I learnt later that this was due to the invasion of thick yellow streams of gas through the voice-pipes from the "Caesar" turret. In the heat of the battle no one had noticed them until suddenly the whole transmitting station was filled with poisonous fumes. The communication officer, Lieutenant Hoch, gave the order: "Connect gunnery apparatus to the forward control," and then he had the transmitting station evacuated. Immediately afterwards brave Artificer Schöning, his gas-mask carefully adjusted re-entered the transmitting station. Feeling his way through the poisonous clouds of gas, with which the place was filled, he reached the voice-pipes and closed them with wooden bungs. Meanwhile the electric ventilators were set going, and in a few minutes the transmitting station began to clear, the gas was drawn off, and the men returned to their stations.

A lull in the fighting was an urgent necessity. At 9.37 p.m. cease fire was ordered, as no enemy ship was now visible. All gun crews were called on deck to put out the fires. The forward bridge was completely enveloped in smoke and flames which the 15-cm. gun crews were set to put out.

The gun fighting had ceased, but now a stub-born struggle was waged against fire and water. Although as far as possible everything inflammable had been taken out of the ship, the fire continued to spread, fed principally by linoleum, the wooden decks, clothing and oil paints. About ten o'clock we had practically mastered the flames, the fire now only smouldering in a few isolated places. The "Caesar" and "Dora" turrets were still smoking and giving out clouds of thick yellow gas from time to time, but this gradually ceased after the ammunition chambers had been flooded. No one could ever have believed that a ship could endure so much heavy fire. The powers of resistance of our ships and the tremendous effectiveness of their fire were a splendid testimony to the builders of our fleet, particularly the brilliant Admiral of the Fleet, von Tirpitz.

The *Lützow* was now lost to sight. At 9.20 p.m. the following was recorded in the after control: "Target covered by thick smoke from the *Lützow*." After this the burning ship had vanished with the ever decreasing visibility.

But the other ships of our squadron, the *Seydlitz*, *Moltke* and *Von der Tann* were still with us. They, too, were in a bad way. The *Seydlitz* had been particularly badly knocked about. On her, too, flames as high as houses leapt out of one gun turret. There were fires on all the ships. The *Seydlitz* was badly down at the bows. When Admiral Hipper came alongside the *Seydlitz* in his destroyer, he was told that all her wireless was out of action, and that she had shipped several thousand tons of water. He therefore tried to board the *Moltke*, commanded by Captain von Karpf, the former captain of the *Hohenzollern*. As he was about to board, the ship came under such a desperate fire that the captain could not reduce speed.

Admiral Hipper then inquired what damage had been sustained by the *Derfflinger*. The following was reported: "Only two 30.5-cm. and two 15-cm. guns still firing on the port side. Three thousand four hundred tons of water in the ship. All signal apparatus destroyed except wireless receiver," whereupon he decided not to transfer his flag to us. As soon as the situation permitted he boarded the *Moltke*, but during all four phases of the battle the battle-cruisers were commanded by the captain of the *Derfflinger*. The name of Captain Hartog is for all time inseparably bound up with the death-ride of the battle-cruisers at Skagerrak.

SKETCH 2

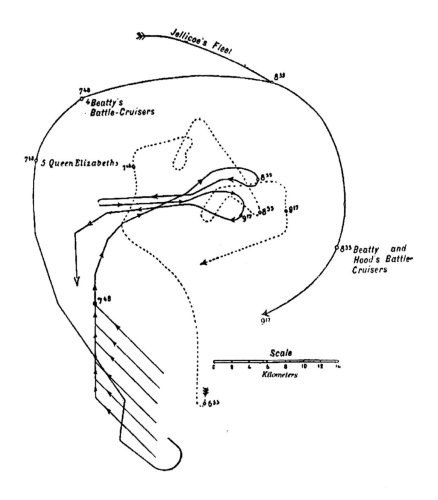

——————— Course of German Battleships.
················· Approximate Course of German Battle-Cruisers.
——————— Course of English Battle-Cruisers and Battleships.

On all our battle-cruisers large numbers of men had been killed. Hundreds had met a hero's death in this proud attack. But our duty of covering, together with the destroyer flotillas, the withdrawal of the fleet had been brilliantly fulfilled. Admiral Scheer was able to withdraw the fleet from the threatened envelopment completely intact.

Sketch 2 shows how the fleet was withdrawn. From this it can be seen that the fleet, in a line of bearing, had steered a north-westerly course until 7.48, and then, in line ahead, north-east until 8.35 p.m. At 8.35 p.m. the fleet once more changed course to the west, but turned again on an easterly course so as not to leave in the lurch the *Wiesbaden*, which was still under heavy fire. At 9.17 p.m. they completed the westerly course ordered at 9.12 and then, covered by the battle-cruisers and destroyer flotillas, withdrew from the semicircular envelopment. From 7.48 p.m. the ships in the van, those of the 3rd Squadron, were engaged by the ships of the *Queen Elizabeth* class.

While steering the easterly courses, which ended at 8.35 p.m. and 9.17 p.m., they also came under the fire of the English main fleet, drawn up in semicircular formation round them. The 1st Squadron in the centre of the line did not come under fire at all during the day's fighting, but in the night-fighting bore the brunt of the battle. The 2nd Squadron, owing to its slow speed, had been left several miles behind. By an accident it took part in the last phase, as I shall describe later. As a result of the correct tactical disposition and leading of our fleet, only our most modern and most powerful ships were engaged by the English ships at the crises of the battle. Only in this way could it have happened that during the battle itself not a single ship was totally lost—the severely damaged *Lützow* was abandoned by her ship's company on the day after the battle and torpedoed by us—whereas the English sacrificed three of their best ships. This fact is brilliant testimony to the perfect tactical skill of Admiral Scheer and his brilliant Chief of Staff, Rear-Admiral von Trotha.

CHAPTER 10

The Fifth Phase of the Skagerrak Battle (9.37 to 10.35 p m and the Night of June 1st

The thrill of our dash straight at the enemy was followed by a lull lasting until 10.22 p.m. In the *Derfflinger* we spent this time making preparations for the night. Nearly all our searchlights had been destroyed. We still had one left on the starboard side and two on the port side. "The Goblin" and his assistants had their hands full to meet even a part of the demands that were made upon them. I remained on the bridge, ready at any moment to engage the enemy. At every periscope a man stood searching the horizon; every telescope was in action.

About 10 p.m. we sighted our 1st Squadron bearing on a southerly course. Our captain, who at this time was commanding the battle-cruisers, led our squadron on the head of our main fleet, where we were to take station. The rest of the battle-cruisers followed the *Derfflinger* without any signal. As we were carrying out this manoeuvre we and the 1st Squadron suddenly came under heavy fire from the south-east. It had already grown dusk. The mist had rather increased than diminished. "Clear for Action!" sounded once more through the ship, and a few seconds later I had trained the "Anna" turret on the target and fired. In the thick mist the "Bertha" turret could not find the target, so I had to fire as well as I could with the "Anna" turret alone. Then this, too, was interrupted. A heavy shell struck the "Anna" turret and bent one of the rails on which the turret revolves, so that it stuck. Our last weapon was snatched out of our hands!

Then *Stückmeister* Weber, with great quickness of decision, ran out of the turret and, with the help of some petty officers and gun hands,

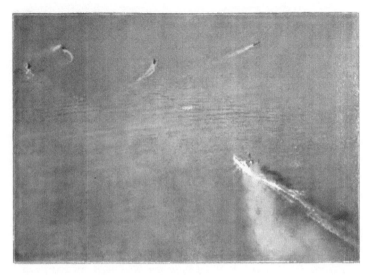

DERFFLINGER SCREENED FROM SUBMARINE ATTACK BY FOUR
DESTROYERS (AERIAL PHOTOGRAPH).

DERFFLINGER FIRING A SALVO FROM HER HEAVY GUNS WHILE
STEAMING AT TOP SPEED (AERIAL PHOTOGRAPH).

cleared away the bent rails with axes and crow-bars and put the turret in action again, so that it was again possible to fire an occasional shot. I had to shoot almost entirely by estimated range, for only rarely was the Bg. man able to get the range of a gun-flash. I fired at ranges of 8,000, 6,000, 1,000, and so on. It was impossible to observe the splashes. The situation had once more become very uncomfortable.

Then help came from the quarter from which it was least expected. After the fleet had turned about on a southerly course our 2nd Squadron, the old ships of the *Deutschland* class, found themselves in the van of the fleet. Admiral Scheer now thought the moment favourable to dispose the fleet in the best tactical formation for the withdrawal south. The 2nd Squadron was therefore ordered to take station astern of the two modern squadrons. The officer commanding the 2nd Squadron was carrying out this manoeuvre at this very moment, bringing his squadron west of the remainder of the fleet and of us. In doing so he came between us and the enemy, who were now pressing us hard. Suddenly the enemy saw seven big ships heading for them at top speed.

At the same time the unwearying destroyers again pressed home the attack. That was too much for them: the enemy turned about and disappeared in the twilight. We did not want to see any more of them, but felt a great relief at this sudden improvement in our situation. I saw all the good friends of my old squadron coming up, the good old *Hessen*, in which I served for five years, the *Pommern*, the *Schleswig-Holstein* and others. They were shooting vigorously and themselves came under a heavy fire. But it was not long before the enemy had had enough. I wonder if they would have turned about had they known what kind of ships these were! They were the famous German "five-minute-ships," to settle which the Englishman could not spare more than five minutes, but bravely withdrew!

At 10.31 p.m. my faithful log-keeper recorded the last shot fired by the *Derfflinger's* heavy guns at an angle of bearing of 244° and a range of 7,500.

The long northern day came to an end. The short night, which only lasted from 11 p.m. to 2 a.m., was beginning.

For the night the battle-cruisers received the order to take station in the rear of the line. We were thus entrusted with the honourable task of covering the rear of the fleet during the withdrawal south. I don't know how the *Seydlitz* and the *Moltke* spent the night. The heavily damaged *Seydlitz* was already having a hard struggle to keep above water. Only by dint of the most strenuous efforts did the crew of this ship, under its efficient commanding officer, Captain von Egidy, and his excellent Second in Command, Commander von Alvensleben, succeed in bringing their ship to Wilhelmshaven two days after the battle.

Only the *Derfflinger* and the *Von der Tann* took station in the rear of the line. We certainly did not feel very well suited to this station. Our starboard was our best side, for it still had all six 15-cm. guns intact. But one single search light was hardly enough. On the port side only two 15-cm. guns were still in action. We should therefore have to urge the English destroyers to confine their attacks as far as possible to the starboard side. There we were still capable of administering a cold douche!

As the sky was overcast the night became very dark. We officers had now left the conning tower for the bridge. The captain came out. He shook me warmly by the hand and said: "Well done!" These words were more to me than any recognition I received later. As it was beginning to get chilly he had a bottle of port wine brought out, the glasses were filled and we drank to the day which was now closing. I sent my servant below to see how things were down there, and to fetch me a fresh overcoat. Hänel came back with the overcoat and reported, beaming: "Your cabin is the only one still ship-shape, sir. All the other cabins are completely wrecked." When I saw his smiling face I couldn't help thinking of the lines:

O heiliger Florian,
Beschütz' mein Haus, zünd' andre an!

As we were the last ship but one in the line we might assume that we should be protected from destroyer attacks, which are nearly always made from ahead. As it turned out, only one English destroyer found her way to us during the whole night. All the other destroyers had been driven off by the ships ahead. About the night fighting I can say little, as we were for the most part well out of it. Firing went on throughout the night. It must be admitted that the English destroyers returned again and again to the attack with amazing pluck. And yet they achieved practically nothing. The only German ship sunk during the night itself was the light cruiser *Frauenlob*, and she was not sunk by the destroyers, but by an English cruiser, which raked her with gunfire and also torpedoed her. Not until dawn did the English destroyers score a success. At very long range one of them succeeded in torpedoing and sinking the *Pommern*.

From our present position we were able to watch undisturbed the fighting which went on for the most part at a considerable distance from us. Searchlights flashed out and lit up the destroyers rushing to the attack. We saw the gun-flashes of ships and destroyers, great splashes were lit by searchlights, thick clouds of smoke drove past the ships and destroyers. We were unable to distinguish details, but the result of the struggle was made clear to us when one blazing, red-hot vessel after another passed us. I could not help thinking of the living torches driven about by the Romans in their orgies of cruelty. All metal parts were aglow and the destroyers looked like fine filigree work in red and gold. The reason for the rapid spread of the fire in the English destroyers lay in the fact that they used only oil fuel. The oil, once alight, spread rapidly over all parts of the pitching vessels. We must have seen quite ten destroyers and other ships dash past us in this way. We watched them with mixed feelings, for we were not quite sure whether any among them were German.

As a matter of fact not a single German destroyer was sunk that night. Our destroyers had gone off to scout for the enemy fleet. It is remark-able, and much to be regretted, that throughout the whole night our destroyers, searching for the great English fleet, failed to find them, although they knew exactly where they were last seen. When the firing ahead had died down a little I heard, as I was standing near the captain, the noise of a turbine destroyer heading for us at full speed on the starboard side. Soon a black object emerged about four points to starboard. Should we use our single searchlight and so betray ourselves, or would it be better to wait until the destroyer's searchlight lit us up to ascertain our position before firing her torpedo?

I quickly suggested to the captain that the searchlight should not be lit. He agreed and the destroyer dashed past us. She was quite near, only 300 to 400 m. away, but she did not show her searchlight and did not fire either her guns or torpedo. Our next astern, the *Von der Tann*, did exactly as we had done. They, too, as the Gunnery Officer told me later, had been afraid that by lighting their searchlights they might draw on themselves the whole destroyer pack. Can the English destroyer not have seen us? Had she already fired all her torpedoes? Had she already been under such heavy fire that her only idea was to get away? I don't know. *Ships that pass in the night.*

This brought the night to a close, and the morning broke. At 2.15 a.m. a burning ship drove past us, the English armoured cruiser *Black*

DERFFLINGER FIRING A FULL SALVO FROM ALL EIGHT 30.5-CM.
GUNS SIMULTANEOUSLY.

AT SEA

Prince. The whole ship was red hot. There could not have been a soul alive on board for some time. At 3.10 a.m. we heard two heavy explosions to port, but could not discover what had happened. We had frequently to stop because the whole line ahead of us was thrown into disorder as a result of the numerous destroyer attacks. To avoid these and to press home counter-attacks, ships were frequently hauling out of the line and steering a circular course, and had to take station again wherever they could. In this way the *Nassau*, originally the second ship of the line, gradually fell into the last place and became our next ahead. It was no light task for our Navigating Officer and Officer of the Watch to keep station at the correct distance astern of the line so that we should not lose touch in the darkness.

When the first signs of dawn appeared we thought it certain that we should again have to engage the whole English fleet. All preparations were made for the day's fighting. The sighting apparatus of the "Bertha" turret had been put in order again by "The Goblin" and his faithful band.

We stood on the bridge forward and searched the darkness and twilight. The destroyer attacks appeared to have ceased. Suddenly—it was about 3.50 a.m.—we heard a heavy explosion, and a mighty tower of flame rose into the sky ahead of us. From the distance it looked like a sheaf of flame from some gigantic firework. We saw our two next ahead put down the helm hard to starboard. What could have happened? What was this new tragedy? Our ship cut her way through the waves as we held on our course, and passed the scene of the disaster. We looked out on all sides for wreckage or men struggling in the water, but there was nothing to be seen. Even as we passed over the actual scene of the catastrophe, we could not realize what had happened. And yet, only a few minutes before, the *Pommern*, a battleship of 13,000 tons, had passed over this same spot.

An English destroyer had crept up to the limit of visibility and torpedoed the *Pommern*. The ship must have been shattered to atoms, as only a few minutes later not the slightest trace of her was to be seen. Not a man of the whole ship's company was saved. My cheery friend and old shipmate, Commander Elle, died like a hero in the *Pommern*. As Gunnery Officer, he had worked with great enthusiasm, and taken great trouble to secure the stowing of ammunition out of danger from torpedoes—now it had been all to no purpose, for obviously the torpedo had hit the magazine direct. It was not till the next day that we learned the name of the ship that had blown up here.

At 4.10 a.m. the 2nd Squadron immediately ahead of us opened fire. We had the "Clear for action" sounded, for we felt sure that now the great decision was to be fought out. But it turned out to be merely an English destroyer that had ventured too near and drawn our fire. It may have been the one that had torpedoed the *Pommern* a short time before. At any rate she had a bad time now. The destroyer, which was not far away from us, was shot into flames, and added one more to the gruesome procession of living torches.

Meanwhile the sun had risen. Hundreds of marine-glasses and periscopes from all our ships scanned the horizon, but no sign of the enemy could be discovered. The fleet held on its southerly course, and in the forenoon of June 1st we ran into Wilhelmshaven.

Our ship was badly knocked about, in some places whole sections were now mere heaps of ruins. The vital parts, however, had not been hit. Thanks to the strong armour, the engines, the boilers, the steering gear, the propeller shafts, and nearly all the auxiliary engines were unharmed. The engine rooms had for some time been filled with poisonous gases, but by using gas-masks the engine room personnel—though they had suffered some losses—had been able to carry on. The whole ship was strewn with thousands of shell-splinters of all sizes. Among these we found two 38-cm. shell caps, almost intact, formidable objects shaped like great bowls, which were used later in the captain's cabin and the wardroom as champagne coolers—though it is to be assumed that this is not the purpose for which the English threw them on board. The armour belt had been pierced in several places, but the holes had all been patched up or the water localized in small compartments.

At Wilhelmshaven we buried our dead, who now lie there in the cemetery of honour. There were nearly two hundred from the *Derfflinger*.

On the 4th June the *Kaiser* inspected our ship, and then she went on the slips at Kiel to be refitted. After numerous gunnery and other improvements we were ready for action again in December, 1916. But the Battle of Skagerrak was our last encounter with the enemy—at least, our last encounter with our flag flying at the mast-head, the flag to which we had sworn our loyalty. Now this proud ship lies with the others on the sea bottom at Scapa Flow.

CHAPTER 11

Reflections on the Battle of Skagerrak

When the sun rose on the 1st June the German fleet lay level with the Horn Reef, on the same meridian of longitude as the Danish town, Esbjerg. As we could then discover no signs of the enemy, far and wide, I confess frankly, a load fell from my heart, for with our battered ship and especially with our decimated armament we should not have been in a position to fight a victorious engagement against one of their heavy battleships with armament intact. I had already fired nearly the whole of the ammunition of "Anna" and "Bertha" turrets and the rest of the ammunition in the "Caesar" and "Dora!" turrets could not be got at, as these turrets were still completely filled with poisonous gases and the ammunition chambers were flooded. For our fleet and our Fatherland I regret from the bottom of my heart that the battle was not fought to a finish.

This fact was certainly a source of great regret and disappointment for our commander-in-chief, Admiral Scheer. It would have been easy for the English to bring us to action in the early morning. Throughout the whole night their cruisers and destroyers had kept in touch with us. All our movements were continually reported by wireless to the English commander-in-chief. It would have been the greatest good fortune for our Fatherland if, at that time, the battle had been reopened off Horn Reef, and so not far from Heligoland. Judging from the experience of the 31st May, many more English ships would have been destroyed, and it would have required an enormous consumption of ammunition to put the German heavy battleships completely out of action.

Had Jellicoe sought a decision off Horn Reef on 1st June there is no doubt that the English fleet would have had to cede its place as the strongest fleet in the world to America.

I admit readily that there was no question of a complete annihilation of Jellicoe's fleet on 1st June. But as one closely acquainted with our ships and our naval guns and also well acquainted with the English ships and their naval guns, and in the light of my gunnery experiences in the Skagerrak battle, I think I can state with certainty that a naval battle fought straight through to a finish between the English and German main fleets would have cost the enemy a very great number of heavy battleships.

On the 31st May it was impossible for Admiral Scheer, after his withdrawal out of the "lion's claws," to bring the fleet afresh into a tactically favourable formation before dawn broke. A night battle between two such powerful fleets was an impossibility. In spite of all identification signals provided for night-fighting a wild melee, a rending of ship against ship without distinction of friend or foe would have been inevitable. But even if we had been reckless enough to seek a night action, the English fleet would have had to avoid it. In a night action they would have had to forgo all the advantages of their preponderating numerical superiority, their greater speed, their long-range guns, and leave everything to blind chance. Jellicoe acted perfectly rightly in disengaging his fleet at nightfall and so skilfully leading his squadron away during the night that our destroyer flotillas, systematically searching the outlying areas of the scene of battle, did not find them.

And Jellicoe also acted perfectly rightly from a strategic point of view in not reopening the battle on the 1st June. The English fleet, by remaining a "fleet in being," by its mere continued existence, had so far fully fulfilled its allotted task. The Battle of Skagerrak did not relax the pressure exerted by the English fleet as a "fleet in being" for one minute. Had Jellicoe on 31st May not accepted the Skagerrak battle, and had he instead, in order to keep his fleet intact, returned to his base at Scapa Flow, we should have been able to carry on our allotted task, war on commerce in the Skagerrak and Kattegatt, and so have kept for a time the naval control of the North Sea. But by the battle of Skagerrak the fulfilment of our task was frustrated. By not attacking on 1st June our fleet heading for the German mine-fields and home ports, Jellicoe kept uninterrupted the mastery of the seas. Why should he, in this strategic game of chess, choose a mutual sacrifice of pieces when his position was such that the mating of the enemy was bound to follow?

Jellicoe returned to Scapa Flow. Later, when he yielded his position as commander-in-chief to Beatty and his king made him a peer, he assumed the name of "Viscount Scapa." At the time there was a good deal of scoffing in Germany, and, indeed, in England too, that an Admiral should take the name of a desolate place where his fleet had remained at anchor almost continuously for four years. And yet by these four years at anchor the English fleet exerted that decisive pressure which ended in our whole fighting fleet being led to this same Scapa Flow where it lies on the sea bottom. What a triumph for the "Viscount of Scapa!"

When, after the Battle of Skagerrak, English belief in their victory had been heavily shaken, Churchill published in the October number of the *London Magazine* a series of articles on the war by land and sea. What he said about the naval war and the battle of Skagerrak is, in my opinion, correct. Alas! it should have taught us the following lesson: The English fleet will only accept battle outside our mine-fields and at a certain respectful distance from our submarine bases and coast defences. But if we are to make any attempt to escape from the iron grip with which England is strangling us we must do all in our power to bring about a naval battle. We must therefore seek out the English fleet off their own coasts and fight them there.

Against this it has been contended that the submarine war could only be carried through so long as our High Sea Fleet remained intact, and that if we had lost our fleet our ports would have been hopelessly blockaded. This argument may be met as follows: In the first place, battle with the enemy fleet was not necessarily synonymous with the loss of our whole fleet. Skagerrak ought to have proved this. And, secondly, in any case we should have been left with enough cruisers, old battleships and destroyers, as well as U-boats, mine-layers, mine-sweepers, airships, aeroplanes and coast defences to carry on the submarine campaign.

Also we should have had the Kattegatt at our disposal as an exit for our U-boats. The submarine campaign in Flanders, where there was no fleet, was carried on in the face of much greater difficulties than we had to contend with in the North Sea. Moreover, a decisive battle on the high seas ought to have made the submarine campaign unnecessary and brought the war to a speedy close.

I do not want these reflections to mar our joy at our partial victory over the English fleet at Skagerrak. But ultimately this victory went the way of all our individual victories on land and sea: it failed to win the final victory for the German nation. At the time, however, it acted on the fleet like a bath of steel, gave the German people new strength and confidence in the future, and added much to the prestige of the German nation. It was a black day for England on which we sent ten thousand English sailors, together with the proudest ships of the English fleet, to the bottom of the sea, while only a few more than two thousand German sailors had to sacrifice their lives under our victorious flag.

I close my account of the greatest day we Germans have ever experienced at sea, with the hope that my little book and Churchill's essay may be the means of enlightening many Germans on the enormous influence that sea power has had on the world's history and will continue to have in the future. I also express the hope that in the years to come many a German, proud of being a German and a sailor, will feel the sea wind whistling past his ears.

Indeed we have become a poor nation. It is true that our national honour has been deeply humiliated. But we will not on that account allow ourselves to be robbed of the courage for fresh deeds. Let us think of the words:

Money lost—Nothing lost!
Honour lost—Much lost!
Courage lost—All lost.

LEONAUR

ALSO FROM LEONAUR

AVAILABLE IN SOFTCOVER OR HARDCOVER WITH DUST JACKET

THE RELUCTANT REBEL *by William G. Stevenson*—A young Kentuckian's experiences in the Confederate Infantry & Cavalry during the American Civil War..

BOOTS AND SADDLES *by Elizabeth B. Custer*—The experiences of General Custer's Wife on the Western Plains.

FANNIE BEERS' CIVIL WAR *by Fannie A. Beers*—A Confederate Lady's Experiences of Nursing During the Campaigns & Battles of the American Civil War.

LADY SALE'S AFGHANISTAN *by Florentia Sale*—An Indomitable Victorian Lady's Account of the Retreat from Kabul During the First Afghan War.

THE TWO WARS OF MRS DUBERLY *by Frances Isabella Duberly*—An Intrepid Victorian Lady's Experience of the Crimea and Indian Mutiny.

THE REBELLIOUS DUCHESS *by Paul F. S. Dermoncourt*—The Adventures of the Duchess of Berri and Her Attempt to Overthrow French Monarchy.

LADIES OF WATERLOO *by Charlotte A. Eaton, Magdalene de Lancey & Juana Smith*—The Experiences of Three Women During the Campaign of 1815: Waterloo Days by Charlotte A. Eaton, A Week at Waterloo by Magdalene de Lancey & Juana's Story by Juana Smith.

TWO YEARS BEFORE THE MAST *by Richard Henry Dana. Jr.*—The account of one young man's experiences serving on board a sailing brig—the Penelope—bound for California, between the years 1834-36.

A SAILOR OF KING GEORGE *by Frederick Hoffman*—From Midshipman to Captain—Recollections of War at Sea in the Napoleonic Age 1793-1815.

LORDS OF THE SEA *by A. T. Mahan*—Great Captains of the Royal Navy During the Age of Sail.

COGGESHALL'S VOYAGES: VOLUME 1 *by George Coggeshall*—The Recollections of an American Schooner Captain.

COGGESHALL'S VOYAGES: VOLUME 2 *by George Coggeshall*—The Recollections of an American Schooner Captain.

TWILIGHT OF EMPIRE *by Sir Thomas Ussher & Sir George Cockburn*—Two accounts of Napoleon's Journeys in Exile to Elba and St. Helena: Narrative of Events by Sir Thomas Ussher & Napoleon's Last Voyage: Extract of a diary by Sir George Cockburn.

LEONAUR

ALSO FROM LEONAUR

AVAILABLE IN SOFTCOVER OR HARDCOVER WITH DUST JACKET

ESCAPE FROM THE FRENCH *by Edward Boys*—A Young Royal Navy Midshipman's Adventures During the Napoleonic War.

THE VOYAGE OF H.M.S. PANDORA *by Edward Edwards R. N. & George Hamilton, edited by Basil Thomson*—In Pursuit of the Mutineers of the Bounty in the South Seas—1790-1791.

MEDUSA *by J. B. Henry Savigny and Alexander Correard and Charlotte-Adélaïde Dard* —Narrative of a Voyage to Senegal in 1816 & The Sufferings of the Picard Family After the Shipwreck of the Medusa.

THE SEA WAR OF 1812 VOLUME 1 *by A. T. Mahan*—A History of the Maritime Conflict.

THE SEA WAR OF 1812 VOLUME 2 *by A. T. Mahan*—A History of the Maritime Conflict.

WETHERELL OF H. M. S. HUSSAR *by John Wetherell*—The Recollections of an Ordinary Seaman of the Royal Navy During the Napoleonic Wars.

THE NAVAL BRIGADE IN NATAL *by C. R. N. Burne*—With the Guns of H. M. S. Terrible & H. M. S. Tartar during the Boer War 1899-1900.

THE VOYAGE OF H. M. S. BOUNTY *by William Bligh*—The True Story of an 18th Century Voyage of Exploration and Mutiny.

SHIPWRECK! *by William Gilly*—The Royal Navy's Disasters at Sea 1793-1849.

KING'S CUTTERS AND SMUGGLERS: 1700-1855 *by E. Keble Chatterton*—A unique period of maritime history-from the beginning of the eighteenth to the middle of the nineteenth century when British seamen risked all to smuggle valuable goods from wool to tea and spirits from and to the Continent.

CONFEDERATE BLOCKADE RUNNER *by John Wilkinson*—The Personal Recollections of an Officer of the Confederate Navy.

NAVAL BATTLES OF THE NAPOLEONIC WARS *by W. H. Fitchett*—Cape St. Vincent, the Nile, Cadiz, Copenhagen, Trafalgar & Others.

PRISONERS OF THE RED DESERT *by R. S. Gwatkin-Williams*—The Adventures of the Crew of the Tara During the First World War.

U-BOAT WAR 1914-1918 *by James B. Connolly/Karl von Schenk*—Two Contrasting Accounts from Both Sides of the Conflict at Sea D uring the Great War.

LEONAUR

ALSO FROM LEONAUR
AVAILABLE IN SOFTCOVER OR HARDCOVER WITH DUST JACKET

FARAWAY CAMPAIGN *by F. James*—Experiences of an Indian Army Cavalry Officer in Persia & Russia During the Great War.

REVOLT IN THE DESERT *by T. E. Lawrence*—An account of the experiences of one remarkable British officer's war from his own perspective.

MACHINE-GUN SQUADRON *by A. M. G.*—The 20th Machine Gunners from British Yeomanry Regiments in the Middle East Campaign of the First World War.

A GUNNER'S CRUSADE *by Antony Bluett*—The Campaign in the Desert, Palestine & Syria as Experienced by the Honourable Artillery Company During the Great War .

DESPATCH RIDER *by W. H. L. Watson*—The Experiences of a British Army Motorcycle Despatch Rider During the Opening Battles of the Great War in Europe.

TIGERS ALONG THE TIGRIS *by E. J. Thompson*—The Leicestershire Regiment in Mesopotamia During the First World War.

HEARTS & DRAGONS *by Charles R. M. F. Crutwell*—The 4th Royal Berkshire Regiment in France and Italy During the Great War, 1914-1918.

INFANTRY BRIGADE: 1914 *by John Ward*—The Diary of a Commander of the 15th Infantry Brigade, 5th Division, British Army, During the Retreat from Mons.

DOING OUR 'BIT' *by Ian Hay*—Two Classic Accounts of the Men of Kitchener's 'New Army' During the Great War including *The First 100,000* & *All In It*.

AN EYE IN THE STORM *by Arthur Ruhl*—An American War Correspondent's Experiences of the First World War from the Western Front to Gallipoli-and Beyond.

STAND & FALL *by Joe Cassells*—With the Middlesex Regiment Against the Bolsheviks 1918-19.

RIFLEMAN MACGILL'S WAR *by Patrick MacGill*—A Soldier of the London Irish During the Great War in Europe including *The Amateur Army*, *The Red Horizon* & *The Great Push*.

WITH THE GUNS *by C. A. Rose & Hugh Dalton*—Two First Hand Accounts of British Gunners at War in Europe During World War 1- Three Years in France with the Guns and With the British Guns in Italy.

THE BUSH WAR DOCTOR *by Robert V. Dolbey*—The Experiences of a British Army Doctor During the East African Campaign of the First World War.

Lightning Source UK Ltd.
Milton Keynes UK
UKOW02f0705260814

237574UK00001B/19/P

9 780857 065940